Contents

INTRODUCTION *1*
How does the Instant Vortex Plus VersaZone Work 1
What to Cook in your Instant Vortex Plus ... 2
How to Use and Clean the Instant Vortex Plus Versa Zone 2
Air Fryer Safety Tips Do's and Don'ts: Mistakes to Avoid 3
Discovering the Benefits of your Instant Vortex Plus 4
Why Every Home Needs an Air Fryer: Health Benefits 4

CHAPTER 1: BREAKFAST *6*
Breakfast Burritos 6
Cinnamon Apple Fritters...................... 6
   Easy Doughnut Muffins 7
Sultana Breakfast Bars 7
Vegetarian Breakfast Casserole 7
   Eggy Bread with Fried Mushrooms 8
Grilled Cheese the British Way 9
Easy Spring Frittata............................ 9
Great British Fry Up 9
Mince Pie Puffs 10
Flapjack Bars with Pecans and Raisins 10
Irish Potato Pancakes (Boxty)................. 11
Scottish Tattie Scones 11
The Fluffiest Crumpets Ever 11
Brioche Breakfast Bake 12
Old-Fashioned Bubble and Squeak........... 12
Bacon Butty (English Bacon Sandwich)...... 13

Baked Bean Omelette 13
Cheesy, savory tortilla pockets 13
Bagels with Cream cheese 14
Nutty, crunchy breakfast blend 14
Hearty Middle Eastern egg dish 15
Spicy Mexican-style eggs 16
Crispy, cinnamon-sugar doughnuts........... 16
Divorced eggs with bold flavors 17
Savory, flaky pastry filled with goodness ... 17
Flavorful, handheld Latin American pies ... 18

CHAPTER 2 : LUNCH *19*
Grandma's Potato Gratin 19
The Easiest British Fish Pie Ever 19
Scottish Rumbledethumps 20
Traditional Beef Wellington 20
Traditional Christmas Turkey 21
Roast Rib of Beef 21
Baked Glazed Ham 21
Roast Pork with Crackling 22
Fish in Ginger-Shallot Sauce 22
Bangers and Mash 23
Vegetarian Cottage Pie 23
Caprese Panini Recipe 24
Mushroom Risotto 24
Italian Wedding Soup 25
Mediterranean Veggie Wrap 25
Chicken Caesar Wrap 26
Buffalo Cauliflower Bites 26
Greek Turkey Burgers 27
Ratatouille 27

Pesto Pasta Salad 28
Vegan Buddha Bowl 28
Tomato and Mozzarella Panini Recipe 29
Pheasant Pie Recipe 29
Chorizo and Red Pepper Tart Recipe 30
Scottish Scallops 30
Cullen Skink Recipe 31
Pheasant Pie Recipe 31
Potted Shrimp Recipe 32

CHAPTER 3: DINNER 33
Cornish Pasty 33
Sausage Ragu 33
Garlic Roast Potatoes 34
Smoked Mackerel Fishcakes 34
Sunday Roast 34
Egg & Chips 35
Salmon in Puff Pastry 35
Toad in the Hole 36
Cauliflower Cheese 36
Steak and Ale Pie 37
Mini Chicken and Mushroom Pies 37
Old-Fashioned Liver and Onions 38
Scampi with Tartare Sauce 38
Butter-Basted Roast Chicken 39
Irish Soda Bread 39
Authentic Glamorgan Sausages 40
Mom's Baked Risotto 40
Country-Style Sausage Casserole 40
Crispy Roast Pork Belly 41
Fish Mornay 42
Tomato Pasta Traybake 42
Vegan Jacket Potatoes 43
The Best Haslet Ever 43
Somerset Chicken 43

Chicken Parmo 44
Chicken Korma 45
Chicken Fettuccine Alfredo 45
Instant Pot Chicken Adobo 46
Instant Pot Pork Carnitas 46
Beef Gyros 47
Chicken Teriyaki 47
Sloppy Joes 48
Corn chowder 48
Chicken Parmesan 49
Baked Ziti 49
Goulash 50
Braised Oxtail Recipe 50
Venison Stew 51
Steak and Stilton Pie 52
Stuffed Bell peppers with Quinoa and Grounded Beef 52
Lentil Soup 53

CHAPTER 4: APPETIZERS 54
Irish Colcannon (Cál Ceannann) 54
Sweet Potato Wedges 54
Devils on Horseback 55
Sausage Rolls 55
British Beef Crostini 55
Roasted Brussels Sprouts 56
Hot Spinach and Artichoke Dip 56
Bourbon Bacon 57
Roasted Asparagus Salad 57
Angels on Horseback 57
Welsh Rarebit 58
Cheese & Onion Pasty 58
Leeks in Cheese Sauce 59
Stilton and Walnut Tarts 59
Spicy Baked Camembert 59

Easy Corn Fritters 60
Classic British Faggots 60
Mashed Peppery Turnips........................ 61
Spicy Parmesan Wafers 61
Roasted Root Vegetables 61
Petite Perfectly Topped Pizza 62
Movie Night Crunchy Popcorn 62
Deliciously Stuffed Ravioli Bites 63
Glazed Heavenly Donut Rings 63
Creamy Tzatziki Dip Recipe 64
Crispy Bread and Butter Pickles.............. 64
Bite-Sized Bagel Delights 65
Crispy Golden Onion Blossoms 65
Crispy Golden Rice Balls 66
Savory Bacon-Wrapped Dates 67
Bite-Sized Quiche Delights.................... 67
Irresistible Mini Corn Dogs 68
Flaky Puff Pastry Pigs in a Blanket 68
Spicy Cheesy Jalapeno Poppers 69
Crispy Seasoned Tater Tots 69

CHAPTER 5: BRITISH CLASSIC ... 70

Rustic pub-style feast 70
Hearty hand-held pie 70
Fragrant, spicy Indian curry 71
Comforting lamb and potato casserole 72
Elegant, savory pastry-wrapped steak........ 72
Toad in the hole 73

Yorkshire Pudding 74
Rich, hearty Irish comfort food 74
Whipped cream and berry delight 75
Sticky Toffee Pudding 75
Buttery, crumbly tea-time treat 76
Moist, tangy citrus dessert 76
Almond and raspberry pastry perfection...... 77
Classic steamed pudding with a playful name
.... 77

CHAPTER 6:DESSERTS 79

Apple Charlotte 79
British Jaffa Cakes 79
Mini Christmas Puddings 80
Classic Yorkies (Yorkshire Puddings)......... 80
Christmas Cake with Brandy Sauce 81
Grandma's Apple Crumble 81
Bread and Butter Pudding 82
Traditional Yorkshire Parkin 82
The Easiest Eccles Cakes Ever 83
Sticky Toffee Pudding........................ 83
St Clement's Pie 84
Mini Rhubarb Crumbles 84
Scottish Shortbread........................... 85
Easy Banana Muffins 85
Gooey Raisin Cookies........................ 86
Chocolate Brownie Cake 86

INTRODUCTION

If you're looking for a healthier and more convenient way to enjoy your favourite foods, then you've come to the right place. The Instant Vortex Plus VersaZone changed the way I cook and eat forever and ever, allowing me to take my culinary art to the next level! I realized that I can use this incredible machine on pretty much everything, from breakfast to snacks and desserts. With its multiple cooking functions, including air frying, baking, roasting, and dehydrating, the possibilities are endless! Plus, I lost a few pounds and managed to reduce high blood pressure along the way. In all modesty, my whole family became much healthier and happier!

The New Instant Vortex Plus Air Fryer Oven Cookbook is your ultimate guide to mastering the art of air frying, with a collection of delicious and easy-to-follow recipes that will take your taste buds on a culinary adventure! Air frying has gained immense popularity in recent years and for good reason. It allows you to enjoy all your favourite fried foods with a fraction of the oil, making them not only healthier but also more guilt-free. But air frying isn't just about making fried foods healthier. It's also a versatile cooking method that can be used for baking, roasting, and even grilling. This Instant Vortex Plus Air Fryer Oven Cookbook for Beginners will show you how to make everything from fluffy flapjacks to juicy steaks using only one kitchen device. Whether you're looking to cook healthier meals, save time in the kitchen, or simply explore new culinary horizons, this cookbook has got you covered. So, let's get started and discover the amazing potential of the Instant Vortex Plus VersaZone!

How does the Instant Vortex Plus VersaZone Work

The Instant Vortex Plus VersaZone is an air fryer and multi-cooker that allows you to cook a variety of foods with hot air circulating them. The Instant Vortex Plus VersaZone is a kitchen appliance that uses circulating hot air to cook food, providing a healthier alternative to traditional deep-frying. Here's how these incredible appliances work:

Heating element – This Air Fryer contains a heating element, similar to a toaster or oven, that heats up the air inside the appliance.

Fan – The heating element is accompanied by a powerful fan that circulates the hot air around the food, creating a convection effect. This ensures that the food is cooked evenly from all sides.

Cooking basket – The food is placed in a cooking basket, which is non-stick and removable. The basket allows the hot air to circulate freely around the food, cooking it from all sides.

Air fryer tray divider and Air fryer cooking tray – You can place your food right on the cooking tray (it means there is no need for foil or baking paper). There is a divider that allows you to cook two different foods at the same time with different temperature and time settings

Temperature and time control – If you want to adjust the cooking time, press "Time" and use the Control Dial to increase or decrease the cooking time. If you want to adjust the cooking temperature, press "Temp" and use the Control Dial to increase or decrease the cooking temperature.

Smart Programmes

You can choose from a variety of cooking modes, including air frying, baking, roasting, broiling, dehydrating, and reheating.

The Instant Vortex Plus VersaZone Air Fryer will allow you to decide how you want to cook and how much, by using different cooking zones – Single Zone and Dual Zone. The machine uses Single zone cooking by default. It is perfect for larger items like Sunday roast or a family-sized batch of chips. Dual Zone will allow you to cook two different items – there are 2 x 4.2 L zones. And the best part – you can switch between Single Zone to Dual Zone! How to do that? Insert the cooking tray into the cooking basket. Add the tray divider to the cooking tray. Put the basket into the unit. Press the Control Dial two times quickly. To switch back to Single Zone cooking, repeat the same steps. That's it!

You can use the SyncCook function to cook different food in both zones at the same time. You can also use the SyncFinish to cook your food in both zones simultaneously and finish cooking at the same time.

What to Cook in your Instant Vortex Plus

The Instant Vortex Plus VersaZone is a versatile kitchen appliance that can be used to cook a variety of foods. Here are some ideas of what you can cook:

Meat and Poultry – It is perfect for making tender meat and crispy cracklings without the added fat from deep frying. Chicken wings turn out great in this magical kitchen device! It can be used to cook pork chops quickly and easily, resulting in a crispy exterior and juicy interior. Instant Vortex Plus VersaZone is perfect for making crispy chicken wings. Simply season them with your favourite spices and cook them for 20 to 25 minutes.

Fish and Seafood – Use your air fryer to cook fish & chips, fish steaks, shellfish, and restaurant-style fish cakes.

Vegetables – You can fry and roast almost all types of vegetables such as broccoli, cauliflower, zucchini, and carrots for a quick and easy side dish or a vegetarian meal. You can make fluffy baked potatoes in a fraction of the time. French fries, jacket potatoes, and roasted potato wedges come out perfect in less than 20 minutes!

Baked goods – The Instant Vortex Plus VersaZone can also be used to bake puff pastries, muffins, and other baked goods. Simply use a baking pan that fits in the air fryer and cook your baked goods according to the recipe.

Vegetarian and Vegan food – For instance, your Instant Vortex Plus VersaZone can make tofu crispy and delicious. Simply season your tofu with your favourite spices and cook it for 10 to 15 minutes. You can also make homemade falafels and cook them in your Air Fryer for a crispy, delicious snack or meal. You can also slice your favourite vegetables thinly and cook them in your Instant Vortex Plus VersaZone for a healthy, crunchy snack. For stuffed peppers, cut the tops off bell peppers and stuff them with your favourite vegetarian filling before cooking in the Air Fryer. The possibilities are endless!

Desserts – Did you know that you can make a wide variety of desserts in your Instant Vortex Plus VersaZone? Believe it or not, it also can be used to make homemade doughnuts, flapjacks, cookies, cakes, and puddings!

How to Use and Clean the Instant Vortex Plus Versa Zone

Here are the basic steps for using the Instant Vortex Plus VersaZone:

- First, read the user manual carefully and ensure that you understand the instructions and safety precautions.
- Preheat the unit according to the instructions in the manual.
- Place your food in the cooking basket, ensuring that it's not overcrowded and has enough space to cook evenly.
- Set the temperature and cooking time according to the recipe or the type of food you're cooking.
- Turn the machine on and let it cook until the timer goes off.
- Once done, turn off the Air Fryer and remove

the basket using the handle.
- Let the cooking basket cool down before serving the food.

It's important to regularly clean your Instant Vortex Plus VersaZone to maintain its performance and prolong its lifespan. Be sure to refer to the user manual for specific instructions and safety precautions.

- First, make sure that the Air Fryer has cooled down before cleaning. Remove the basket and any other removable parts and wash them in warm, soapy water. Avoid using abrasive cleaners or utensils that can scratch the non-stick coating.
- Use a soft sponge or cloth to wipe down the interior of the Instant Vortex Plus VersaZone, being careful not to damage the heating element. If there is any stubborn residue or grease, you can use a non-abrasive sponge or a cleaning solution made specifically for air fryers.
- Wipe the exterior of the Air Fryer with a damp cloth or sponge. Dry all parts thoroughly before reassembling the Air Fryer.
- Store your Instant Vortex Plus VersaZone in a dry and safe place.

Air Fryer Safety Tips Do's and Don'ts: Mistakes to Avoid

By following certain safety tips, you can use your Instant Vortex Plus VersaZone to cook delicious and healthy meals without any accidents or mishaps. Here are some do's and don'ts to keep in mind:

Do's:
- Read the instruction manual carefully before using your Instant Vortex Plus VersaZone.
- Place the air fryer on a flat, heat-resistant surface to prevent it from tipping over.
- Keep the air fryer away from the edge of the counter and out of reach of children.
- Use oven mitts or silicone gloves when handling the basket or tray to avoid burns.
- Clean your Instant Vortex Plus VersaZone regularly to prevent the buildup of grease and food residue.
- Use the Instant Vortex Plus VersaZone in a well-ventilated area to avoid setting off smoke alarms.
- Use the right amount of oil or cooking spray as recommended in the recipe.
- Use a food thermometer to ensure that the food is cooked to the appropriate temperature.

Don'ts:
- Never use the Instant Vortex Plus VersaZone without the basket or tray in place.
- Do not overcrowd the basket or tray as this can affect the cooking time and result in unevenly cooked food.
- Do not use metal utensils or abrasive cleaning tools on the non-stick coating of the basket or tray.
- Do not use aerosol cooking sprays or oils as they can damage the non-stick coating and create a fire hazard.
- Do not use the air fryer to cook foods that are wet or have a high moisture content, such as raw batter or wet dough.
- Do not leave the air fryer unattended while it is in use.
- Do not touch the heating element or interior of the air fryer while it is hot.
- Do not immerse the air fryer in water or other liquids.

Here are seven things you should avoid cooking in the Instant Vortex Plus VersaZone:

Raw Batter – Air fryers are not suitable for cooking raw batter, such as that used for onion rings or tempura. The batter can drip through the basket and onto the heating element, causing smoke and a potential fire hazard. Also, avoid cooking foods with loose toppings, such as grated cheese or breadcrumbs; loose toppings may fly around the air fryer and cause a mess or get stuck on the heating element.

Cheese – Air fryers are not the best choice for cooking foods with a lot of cheese, such as pizza.

The cheese can melt and drip through the basket, causing a mess and potentially damaging the heating element.

Delicate Vegetables – Delicate vegetables such as greens and beans may become too dry and lose their texture when cooked in an air fryer.

Wet Batters – Air fryers are not ideal for cooking foods with wet batters, such as chicken wings. The batter can drip through the basket and onto the heating element, causing smoke and a potential fire hazard.

Canned Foods – Air fryers are not recommended for cooking canned foods, such as soups or stews. The high heat and fast cooking time can cause the can to explode and potentially harm the user.

Foods with High Water Content – Foods that have a high-water content, such as watery fruits or vegetables, may release too much moisture and cause the air fryer to smoke or steam.

Raw Grains – When you cook raw grains in an air fryer, you run the risk of burning or scorching the grains, as air fryers use a high temperature and dry heat to cook food. Additionally, without the necessary liquid, the grains may not cook evenly or become too dry, resulting in a less-than-desirable texture and taste.

Discovering the Benefits of your Instant Vortex Plus

We usually think that bringing nutritious and delicious meals to the table requires some special skills and struggling in the kitchen. This couldn't be further from the truth! All that's required is a change in your cooking habits! The Instant Vortex Plus VersaZone is a versatile kitchen appliance that can be used for various cooking functions. Some of the benefits of using this appliance include:

Versatility – The Instant Vortex Plus VersaZone can be used for various cooking functions, including air frying, roasting, baking, broiling, dehydrating, and reheating. This versatility means that you can cook a wide range of foods with this appliance.

Quick Cooking – The Instant Vortex Plus VersaZone uses Rapid Air Technology to cook food quickly and evenly. This technology circulates hot air around the food, resulting in crispy and evenly cooked meals in a short amount of time. With this incredible machine, homemade, freshly-prepared meals are just minutes away!

Easy to Use – The Instant Vortex Plus VersaZone is designed with easy-to-use controls and a digital display. This makes it easy to select the cooking function, temperature, and time for your meal.

Easy to Clean – The Instant Vortex Plus VersaZone is designed with a non-stick interior, which makes it easy to clean after cooking. The appliance also comes with dishwasher-safe accessories, making cleanup even easier.

Saves Space – The Instant Vortex Plus VersaZone is a multi-functional appliance that can replace several other kitchen appliances, such as a toaster oven, microwave, and deep fryer. This means that it can save you valuable counter and storage space in your kitchen.

Healthier Cooking – The Instant Vortex Plus VersaZone uses hot air frying technology, which means that it requires little to no oil to cook food. This results in healthier meals that are lower in fat and calories.

Why Every Home Needs an Air Fryer: Health Benefits

Lower fat intake – The Instant Vortex Plus VersaZone use hot air circulation to cook food instead of oil. This means that you can cook your favourite fried foods with up to 80% less oil, reducing your overall fat intake.

Reduced calorie intake – With less oil used in cooking, the calorie content of your food is also reduced. This makes air fryers an excellent option for individuals looking to maintain a healthy weight.

Lower risk of heart disease – Consuming too much oil in your diet can increase your risk of heart disease. Air fryers can help reduce your intake of unhealthy fats, which can lower your risk of developing heart disease.

Healthier food choices – The Instant Vortex Plus VersaZone can help make healthier food choices easier by allowing you to cook foods such as vegetables and lean meats without the need for excess oil.

Reduced acrylamide formation – When certain foods are cooked at high temperatures, they can form acrylamide, which has been linked to an increased risk of cancer. The Instant Vortex Plus VersaZone cooks food at a lower temperature, reducing the formation of acrylamide.

So, are you ready to revamp your cooking style? This cookbook is your ultimate guide to cooking delicious and healthy meals using the Instant Vortex Plus VersaZone. With these 90 delicious and healthy recipes, you'll never look at fried food the same way again.

This cookbook is designed to introduce you to the basics of using the Instant Vortex Plus VersaZone and help you become a pro in no time. This cookbook is packed with delicious and easy-to-make recipes that will make you fall in love with your air fryer all over again. Whether you're a seasoned pro or just starting out, you'll find something to tantalize your taste buds and inspire your culinary creativity. So fire up your Instant Vortex Plus VersaZone, and let's get cooking!

CHAPTER 1: BREAKFAST

Breakfast Burritos

Serves 4
Prep time: 10 minutes
Cook time: 10 minutes

Ingredients

- 1 tbsp olive oil
- 400g breakfast sausages, sliced
- 250g brown mushrooms, sliced
- 1 tsp Taco seasoning mix
- 2 small red peppers, finely sliced
- 4 large tortilla wraps

Tomato Salsa:
- 2 medium vine tomatoes, chopped
- 1 small red chilli, deseeded and minced
- 2 tbsp fresh coriander, finely chopped
- 1/2 small red onion, finely chopped
- 1/2 lime, juiced

Instructions

1. Slide the tray divider into the cooking tray. Put the cooking basket into the Air Fryer and then, press the Control Dial two times quickly to activate Dual Zone cooking.
2. Toss breakfast sausages and mushrooms with olive oil and Taco seasoning mix. Lower the sausages into Drawer 1 of your Air Fryer.
3. Select "Air Fry" on this drawer and set the temperature to 200 degrees C and the time to 10 minutes.
4. Place the prepared mushrooms in Drawer 2. Select "Air Fry", and set the temperature to 180 degrees C and the time to 7 minutes. Select "SyncFinish" to ensure both drawers finish at the same time.
5. When the display shows "Turn Food", remove the cooking basket and carefully flip your food. Insert the basket again to continue cooking.
6. Whilst sausage and mushrooms cook, make the salsa: combine all of the Ingredients; season to taste.
7. To assemble your burritos: divide fried breakfast sausages, mushrooms, and peppers, between tortilla wraps; top them with the freshly prepared salsa.
8. Lastly, wrap them up and serve. Enjoy!

Cinnamon Apple Fritters

Serves 4
Prep time: 10 minutes
Cook time: 13 minutes

Ingredients

- 2 medium apples, peeled
- 1 tsp freshly squeezed lemon juice
- 200g oat flour
- 100g golden caster sugar
- A pinch of grated nutmeg
- A pinch of sea salt
- 1 tsp baking powder
- 1 tsp cinnamon powder
- 1 medium egg, beaten
- 120ml cup coconut milk
- 1 tsp coconut oil

Instructions

1. Core your apples and slice them into rings. Toss the apple ring in the lemon juice to stop them from going brown.
2. Then, thoroughly combine the oat flour, sugar, nutmeg, salt, baking powder, and cinnamon.
3. In a separate bowl, whisk the egg with coconut milk. To make a batter, add the wet mixture to the dry Ingredients; mix to combine well.
4. Dip apple rings into the batter; arrange them in the Air Fryer cooking basket that is

previously greased with coconut oil.
5. Cook the apple fritters at 185 degrees C for about 13 minutes, turning them over halfway through the cooking time. Work in batches.
6. When the display shows "Turn Food", remove the cooking basket and carefully flip your apple fritters. Insert the basket again to continue cooking.
7. Serve the apple fritters with powdered sugar, if used. Bon appétit!

Easy Doughnut Muffins

Serves 6
Prep time: 10 minutes
Cook time: 16 minutes

Ingredients
- 100 g plain flour
- 1/2 tsp baking powder
- 1/2 tsp bicarbonate of soda
- 170 g golden caster sugar
- 1 large egg, beaten
- 50ml full-fat yoghurt
- A pinch of sea salt
- A pinch of grated nutmeg
- 1/2 tsp ground cinnamon
- 1/2 tsp vanilla extract
- 50g butter, melted
- 6 tsp jam of choice

Instructions
1. Lightly grease a 6-hole muffin tin using cooking spray.
2. In a mixing bowl, thoroughly combine the flour, baking powder, bicarb, and 70g of sugar.
3. In a separate jug, whisk the eggs, yoghurt, and spices until frothy. Add the melted butter and whisk again. Tip the jug contents into the dry mixture; stir to combine well.
4. Divide 2/3 of the batter between muffin holes. Spoon 1 tsp of your favourite jam into the centre of each muffin; cover them with the remaining 1/3 of the batter.
5. Select "Bake" and set the time for 16 minutes and the temperature to 200 degrees C. Leave doughnut muffins to cool for about 7 minutes before unmolding.
6. Roll warm doughnut muffins over the remaining 100 grams of sugar and serve. Bon appétit!

Sultana Breakfast Bars

Prep time: 10 minutes
Cook time: 16 minutes
Serves 10

Ingredients
- 50g multi-grain cereal
- 160g instant oats
- 120g coconut oil, softened
- 120g golden caster sugar
- 100g maple syrup
- 50g sultanas
- 30g hemp seed, hulled
- 20g pumpkin seeds

Instructions
1. Thoroughly combine all Ingredients in a bowl. Line a cooking tray with a piece of baking parchment.
2. Spoon the mixture into the prepared baking tray; press down the mixture with a wide spatula.
3. Select "Bake" and set the time for 16 minutes and the temperature to 180 degrees C.
4. Leave it to cool before slicing it into bars.
5. Bon appétit!

Vegetarian Breakfast Casserole

Serves 5
Prep time: 10 minutes
Cook time: 22 minutes

Ingredients

- 300g chestnut mushrooms, sliced
- 1 bell pepper, deseeded and sliced
- 1 medium carrot, thinly sliced
- 1 small onion, thinly sliced
- 1 tsp dried oregano
- 1 tsp dried basil
- 1 tsp dried rosemary
- 1/2 tsp cayenne pepper
- Sea salt and ground black pepper, to taste
- 200g vegetarian sausages, sliced into bite-sized chunks
- 2 tsp olive oil
- 1 large red onion, finely sliced
- 7 eggs
- 200ml whole milk
- 100g Parmesan cheese, preferably freshly grated
- 1 tbsp fresh parsley, chopped

Instructions

1. Slide the tray divider into the cooking tray and press the Control Dial two times quickly to activate Dual Zone cooking.
2. Toss your mushrooms, peppers, carrots, and onion with spices and 1 teaspoon of olive oil. Arrange your vegetables on the baking tray.
3. Lower the vegetables into Drawer 1 of your Air Fryer. Select "Roast" on this drawer and set the temperature to 180 degrees C and the time to 7 minutes. Place the sausages in Drawer 2.
4. Select "SyncCook" to automatically mirror the settings in Drawer 2. Reserve the vegetables and sausages.
5. Wipe down the interior of your Air Fryer. Brush the interior of a casserole dish (or four ramekins) with the remaining 1 teaspoon of olive oil.
6. Spoon the vegetables and sausages into the prepared casserole dish (or ramekins).
7. Whisk the remaining Ingredients and spoon the topping mixture over your vegetables and sausages.
8. Select "Bake" and set the time for 15 minutes and the temperature to 180 degrees C.
9. When the display shows "Turn Food", remove the cooking basket and carefully rotate the casserole. Insert the cooking basket again to continue cooking.
10. Bon appétit!

Eggy Bread with Fried Mushrooms

Prep time: 5 minutes
Cook time: 7 minutes
Serves 2

Ingredients

- 2 medium eggs
- 1 tbsp plain milk
- Himalayan salt and ground black pepper, to taste
- 2 tsp olive oil
- 4 slices of brown bread
- 200g button mushrooms, sliced

Instructions

1. Beat the egg and milk in a shallow bowl. Add the salt and black pepper to taste, and beat again until pale and frothy.
2. Slide the tray divider into the cooking tray and press the Control Dial two times quickly to activate Dual Zone cooking.
3. Lower the eggy bread into Drawer 1 of your Air Fryer. Brush them with 1 teaspoon of olive oil. Select "Air Fry" on this drawer and set the temperature to 185 degrees C and the time to 7 minutes.
4. Toss the sliced mushrooms with salt, black pepper, and the remaining 1 teaspoon of olive oil. Place the mushrooms in Drawer 2.
5. Select "SyncCook" to automatically mirror

the settings in Drawer 2. When the display shows "Turn Food", remove the cooking basket and carefully turn each slice of bread over. Insert the basket again to continue cooking until golden brown.
6. Serve warm eggy bread with fried mushrooms on the side and enjoy!

Grilled Cheese the British Way

Prep time: 5 minutes
Cook time: 10 minutes
Serves 3

Ingredients
- 3 tsp butter
- 6 thin slices of brown bread
- 60g cheddar cheese, grated
- Ground black pepper, to taste
- 3 rashers streaky bacon

Instructions
1. Butter one side of each slice of bread.
2. Divide the cheese between 3 slices of bread (on the unbuttered side). Season with black pepper to taste. Top with another slice of bread (buttered-side up).
3. Slide the tray divider into the cooking tray and press the Control Dial two times quickly to activate Dual Zone cooking.
4. Arrange your toasties in Drawer 1 of your Air Fryer. Select "Bake" on this drawer and set the temperature to 180 degrees C and the time to 10 minutes.
5. Place the bacon in Drawer 2. Select "Air Fry", and set the temperature to 180 degrees C and the time to 6 minutes. Select "SyncFinish" to ensure both drawers finish at the same time.
6. When the display shows "Turn Food", remove the cooking basket and carefully flip the toasties and bacon over. Insert the basket again to continue cooking. Serve immediately and enjoy!

Easy Spring Frittata

Prep time: 5 minutes
Cook time: 22 minutes
Serves 4

Ingredients
- 300g new potatoes, diced
- 2 spring onions, chopped
- 200g asparagus tips
- 1 tbsp olive oil
- 7 eggs, beaten
- 50g Parmesan cheese, preferably freshly grated
- Sea salt and ground black pepper, to taste
- 1 tsp dried rosemary
- 1 tsp dried thyme

Instructions
1. Add new potatoes to the Air Fryer cooking tray. Select "Air Fry"; set the temperature to 180 degrees C and the time to 12 minutes.
2. Meanwhile, mix the other Ingredients until everything is well incorporated. Next, fold in the potatoes and gently stir to combine.
3. Spoon the mixture into a lightly greased baking tray and add it to the Air Fryer cooking basket.
4. Select "Bake", and set the temperature to 200 degrees C and the time to 10 minutes.
5. Bon appétit!

Great British Fry Up

Prep time: 5 minutes
Cook time: 9 minutes
Serves 2

Ingredients
- 2 small tomatoes, halved

- 200g brown mushrooms, cut into quarters
- 1 tsp olive oil
- 1/2 tsp cayenne pepper
- Sea salt and ground black pepper, to taste
- 5 rashers back bacon
- 4 links breakfast sausage
- 100g canned baked beans, drained

Instructions

1. Toss the tomatoes and mushrooms with olive oil, cayenne pepper, salt, and black pepper.
2. Slide the tray divider into the cooking tray and press the Control Dial two times quickly to activate Dual Zone cooking.
3. Arrange vegetables along with bacon in Drawer 1 of your Air Fryer. Select "Air Fry" on this drawer and set the temperature to 180 degrees C and the time to 9 minutes.
4. Place the sausages in Drawer 2. Select "Air Fry", and set the temperature to 180 degrees C and the time to 6 minutes. Select "SyncFinish" to ensure both drawers finish at the same time.
5. Serve vegetables, sausage, and bacon with canned beans. Add black pudding and fried eggs (optional) for a complete Great British Fry Up. Enjoy!

Mince Pie Puffs

Prep time: 10 minutes
Cook time: 15 minutes
Serves 6

Ingredients

- 1 (320g) sheet puff pastry
- 200g mincemeat
- 1 tsp butter
- 1 medium egg, beaten
- 2 tbsp powdered sugar

Instructions

1. On a lightly floured working surface, roll the sheet of puff pastry out using a rolling pin. Now, cut circles into the pastry with a cookie cutter.
2. Divide the mincemeat mixture between 1/2 of the circles. Lay the other circles on top and press to seal. Brush them with melted butter.
3. Brush mini pies with beaten egg and arrange them on the cooking tray.
4. Select "Bake", and set the temperature to 180 degrees C and the time to 15 minutes.
5. Lastly, dust warm pies with powdered sugar and enjoy!

Flapjack Bars with Pecans and Raisins

Prep time: 5 minutes
Cook time: 20 minutes
Serves 6

Ingredients

- 70g butter, melted
- 90g brown soft sugar
- 150g instant oats
- 2 tbsp pecans, chopped
- 50g raisins

Instructions

1. Line the Air Fryer cooking tray with a piece of baking paper.
2. Mix the Ingredients until everything is well incorporated.
3. Tip the batter into the prepared Air Fryer tray and press down with the back of a spoon.
4. Select "Bake"; set the temperature to 180 degrees C and the time to 20 minutes. There is no need to rotate the cooking tray.
5. Leave to cool for about 10 minutes before cutting into 6 flapjacks.
6. Bon appétit!

Irish Potato Pancakes (Boxty)

Prep time: 5 minutes
Cook time: 25 minutes
Serves 4

Ingredients

- 2 raw potatoes, grated
- 100g mashed potatoes
- 100g plain flour
- 1 large egg
- 1 tbsp plain milk
- 1 tsp paprika
- 1/2 tsp garlic granules
- Sea salt and ground black pepper, to taste
- 1 tbsp butter

Instructions

1. In a mixing bowl, thoroughly combine grated potatoes, mashed potatoes, and flour.
2. In a separate bowl, whisk the egg and milk until pale and frothy; stir the egg mixture into the potato mixture. Season with paprika, garlic granules, salt, and black pepper.
3. Shape the mixture into patties and arrange them on the cooking tray. Brush your patties with melted butter.
4. Select "Air Fry"; set the temperature to 200 degrees C and the time to 25 minutes.
5. When the display shows "Turn Food", remove the cooking basket and carefully flip your patties over. Insert the basket again to continue cooking.
6. For a traditional Irish dish, serve your Boxty with bacon and sour cream, if desired. Bon appétit!

Scottish Tattie Scones

Prep time: 5 minutes
Cook time: 35 minutes
Serves 6

Ingredients

- 500g new potatoes, scrubbed
- 25g butter, softened
- 1/2 tsp cayenne pepper
- Sea salt and ground black pepper, to taste
- 120g plain flour (plus more for rolling)

Instructions

1. Add new potatoes to the Air Fryer cooking tray. Select "Air Fry"; set the temperature to 200 degrees C and the time to 15 minutes.
2. Mash the potatoes and add the other Ingredients. Mix until a dough ball forms.
3. Turn the prepared dough out onto a lightly floured surface and separate it into 2 balls.
4. Pat each ball out into a flat circle, turning and lightly flouring each side so that it doesn't stick. Prick both circles all over with a fork and place them on a parchment-lined cooking tray.
5. Select "Bake", and set the temperature to 180 degrees C and the time to 20 minutes.
6. When the display shows "Turn Food", remove the cooking basket and carefully flip the scones over. Insert the basket again to continue cooking.
7. Serve with toppings of choice and enjoy!

The Fluffiest Crumpets Ever

Prep time: 10 minutes
Cook time: 16 minutes
Serves 6

Ingredients

- 1 tsp dried yeast
- 100ml warm water
- 150ml warm milk
- 1 tbsp butter, melted
- 1 tsp sea salt
- 1 tsp golden caster sugar
- A pinch of ground cinnamon

- A pinch of ground cardamom
- 230g plain flour
- 1/2 tsp baking powder
- 1 tsp olive oil

Instructions

1. In a bowl, mix the yeast and warm water, and let it stand for about 10 minutes.
2. Add the other Ingredients and stir until uniform and smooth. Leave the batter to rest for about 30 minutes.
3. Spoon the batter into a muffin tin.
4. Select "Bake" and set the time for 16 minutes and the temperature to 200 degrees C. Leave your crumpets to cool for about 7 minutes before unmolding and serving.
5. Good serving options include cheese, some extra butter, and sour cream.
6. Bon appétit!

Brioche Breakfast Bake

Prep time: 10 minutes + chilling time
Cook time: 15 minutes
Serves 6

Ingredients

- 160ml double cream
- 4 large eggs
- 250ml plain milk
- 1/4 tsp ground cinnamon
- A pinch of sea salt
- 1 tsp vanilla extract
- 200g raisins
- 9 brioche rolls, split in half
- 60g almond, slivered
- 50g icing sugar, for dusting

Instructions

1. Whisk the cream, eggs, milk, cinnamon, sea salt, and vanilla.
2. Then, add the raisins, brioche rolls, and almonds to a lightly buttered casserole dish. Spoon the custard mixture into the casserole dish.
3. Cover this dish with cling film and place it in your fridge for about 1 hour. Place the casserole dish in the cooking basket.
4. Select "Bake" and set the time for 15 minutes and the temperature to 180 degrees C.
5. When the display shows "Turn Food", remove the cooking basket and carefully rotate the casserole. Insert the cooking basket again to continue cooking.
6. Dust your casserole with icing sugar just before serving.
7. Bon appétit!

Old-Fashioned Bubble and Squeak

Prep time: 10 minutes
Cook time: 30 minutes
Serves 5

Ingredients

- 500g potatoes, peeled and cut into wedges
- 1 tbsp lard
- 1 garlic clove, chopped
- 4 rashers back bacon, chopped
- 200g Brussels sprouts, chopped
- 200g kale, chopped
- 1 small leek, chopped
- 1 rosemary sprig, chopped
- 1 thyme sprig, chopped
- Sea salt and ground black pepper, to taste
- 1/2 tsp cayenne pepper

Instructions

1. Add potatoes to the Air Fryer cooking tray. Select "Air Fry", and set the temperature to 200 degrees C and the time to 15 minutes.
2. Mash the potatoes and add the other Ingredients. Now, press the mixture into a parchment-lined Air Fryer cooking tray.
3. Select "Bake" and set the time for 15 minutes

and the temperature to 200 degrees C.
4. When the display shows "Turn Food", remove the cooking basket and rotate your bubble and squeak together with baking paper. Insert the basket again to continue cooking.
5. Bon appétit!

Bacon Butty (English Bacon Sandwich)

Prep time: 5 minutes
Cook time: 15 minutes
Serves 4

Ingredients
- 8 rachers back bacon
- 4 crusty rolls
- A few drizzles of Worcestershire sauce
- 4 tbsp ketchup

Instructions
1. Arrange rashers of bacon in the Air Fryer cooking basket.
2. Select "Air Fryer" and set the time for 9 minutes and the temperature to 190 degrees C.
3. Place the bacon slices inside crusty rolls to create a sandwich.
4. Add Worcestershire sauces and ketchup. Place your sandwiches in the Air Fryer cooking basket
5. Toast your sandwiches: Select "Air Fryer" and set the time for 6 minutes and the temperature to 180 degrees C. Serve immediately and enjoy!

Baked Bean Omelette

Prep time: 5 minutes
Cook time: 12 minutes
Serves 2

Ingredients
- 4 eggs
- 4 tbsp plain milk
- 1 small bell pepper, deseeded and chopped
- 2 cloves garlic, minced
- 1 tbsp fresh parsley leaves, chopped
- 2 tbsp fresh chives, chopped
- 1 tsp cayenne pepper
- Sea salt and ground black pepper, to taste
- 1 can of refried beans
- 4 tbsp Cheddar cheese, grated

Instructions
1. In a mixing bowl, beat the eggs with milk until frothy. Add the chopped pepper, garlic, herbs, and spices.
2. Fold in the canned beans and gently stir to combine.
3. Line a baking tray with baking paper. Pour the omelette mixture into the prepared baking tray.
4. Select "Air Fryer" and set the time for 9 minutes and the temperature to 200 degrees C. Top your omelette with cheese and let it cook for 3 minutes, until the cheese melts.
5. Slide off the omelette onto a plate using a wide spatula. Cut into 2 halves. Bon appétit!

Cheesy, savory tortilla pockets

Serves :4
Prep time: 15 minutes
Cook time: 20 minutes

Ingredients:
- 4 large flour tortillas (25cm)
- 200g of shredded cheddar cheese
- 150g of cooked chicken, shredded
- 15g chopped fresh cilantro
- 70g of diced tomatoes
- 70g of diced red onions
- 60ml of olive oil

Instructions
1. Preheat the Instant Vortex Plus Versa Zone to

180°C.
2. In a medium-sized bowl, mix together the shredded cheese, cooked chicken, cilantro, diced tomatoes, and diced red onions.
3. Place a tortilla on a flat surface, and spread 1/4 of the cheese and chicken mixture on one half of the tortilla.
4. Fold the tortilla over, and press down firmly.
5. Repeat with the remaining tortillas and cheese and chicken mixture.
6. Brush each quesadilla with olive oil on both sides.
7. Place the quesadillas in the Instant Vortex Plus Versa Zone and cook for 10 minutes on each side, or until the tortillas are crispy and golden brown.
8. Remove the quesadillas from the Instant Vortex Plus Versa Zone and let them cool for 1-2 minutes before slicing into wedges.
9. Serve hot with your favorite toppings, such as sour cream, salsa, or guacamole.

Bagels with Cream cheese

Serves: 4
Prep time: 20 minutes
Cook time: 15 minutes

Ingredients:

For the Bagels:
- 300g all-purpose flour
- 1 tsp salt
- 1 tsp sugar
- 1 tsp instant yeast
- 180ml warm water
- 1 egg, beaten
- Sesame seeds or poppy seeds (optional)

For the Cream Cheese:
- 200g cream cheese
- 60ml heavy cream
- 1 tbsp honey
- 1/4 tsp salt

Instructions

1. In a large mixing bowl, whisk together the flour, salt, sugar, and instant yeast.
2. Add the warm water to the dry Ingredients and mix until a dough forms. Knead the dough on a floured surface for about 5 minutes, or until smooth and elastic.
3. Divide the dough into 4 equal pieces and shape each piece into a ball. Use your finger to poke a hole in the center of each ball and stretch the hole until it's about 1-2 inches wide.
4. Place the bagels on a parchment-lined baking sheet and let them rise for about 10-15 minutes.
5. Preheat your Instant Vortex Plus Versa Zone air fryer to 180°C
6. Brush the beaten egg over the tops of the bagels and sprinkle with sesame seeds or poppy seeds, if desired.
7. Place the bagels in the instant Vortex Plus Versa Zone basket and cook for 12-15 minutes, or until golden brown and cooked through.
8. While the bagels are cooking, make the cream cheese. In a mixing bowl, combine the cream cheese, heavy cream, honey, and salt. Mix until smooth and creamy.
9. Once the bagels are done, let them cool for a few minutes before slicing them in half.
10. Spread the cream cheese mixture on the bagel halves and enjoy

Nutty, crunchy breakfast blend

Serves: 4-6
Prep time: 5 minutes/ Cook time: 15 minutes

Ingredients:
- 200g old-fashioned rolled oats
- 50g chopped almonds

- 50g chopped pecans
- 30g unsweetened coconut flakes
- 30g dried cranberries or raisins
- 1/4 tsp salt
- 1/4 tsp cinnamon
- 60ml maple syrup
- 30ml coconut oil, melted
- 1 tsp vanilla extract

Instructions

1. In a mixing bowl, combine the oats, chopped almonds, chopped pecans, coconut flakes, dried cranberries or raisins, salt, and cinnamon.
2. In a separate bowl, whisk together the maple syrup, melted coconut oil, and vanilla extract.
3. Pour the liquid mixture over the oat mixture and stir until everything is well-coated.
4. Preheat your Instant Vortex Plus Versa Zone air fryer to 165°C
5. Spread the granola mixture evenly on the Instant Vortex Plus Versa Zone basket.
6. Cook for 10-15 minutes, or until the granola is golden brown and crispy, stirring every 5 minutes to prevent burning.
7. Once done, let the granola cool completely before transferring it to an airtight container.
8. Serve as desired, either as a topping for yogurt, with milk or on its own

Hearty Middle Eastern egg dish

Serves: 2-3
Prep time: 10 minutes
Cook time: 15 minutes

Ingredients:

- 1 tbsp (15ml) of olive oil
- 1/2 onion, chopped
- 1 red bell pepper, chopped
- 2 garlic cloves, minced
- 2g of paprika
- 2g of cumin
- 400g of diced tomatoes
- 60ml of water
- Salt and pepper, to taste
- 3-4 eggs
- Optional toppings: feta cheese, chopped parsley, pita bread

Instructions

1. Preheat your Instant Vortex Plus Versa Zone air fryer to 190°C
2. Heat the olive oil in a skillet over medium heat.
3. Add the chopped onion and red bell pepper to the skillet and cook for 5-7 minutes, or until softened.
4. Add the minced garlic, paprika, and cumin to the skillet and cook for another minute, stirring frequently.
5. Pour the can of diced tomatoes and water into the skillet and stir to combine.
6. Season the mixture with salt and pepper to taste.
7. Once the mixture is heated through, transfer it to a baking dish that fits into the Instant Vortex Plus Versa Zone basket.
8. Use a spoon to make 3-4 wells in the tomato mixture.
9. Crack an egg into each well.
10. Place the baking dish in the Instant Vortex Plus Versa Zone basket and cook for 10-15 minutes, or until the egg whites are set but the yolks are still runny.
11. Once done, remove the baking dish from the Instant Vortex and let it cool for a few minutes.
12. Serve the Shakshuka with any desired toppings, such as crumbled feta cheese, chopped parsley, or pita bread.

Spicy Mexican-style eggs

Serves: 2
Prep time: 10 minutes
Cook time: 10 minutes

Ingredients:
- 4 corn tortillas
- 4 eggs
- 1 can (400g) of black beans, drained and rinsed
- 1/2 cup (125ml) of salsa
- 1/2 cup (50g) of shredded cheddar cheese
- 2 tbsp (30ml) of vegetable oil
- Salt and pepper, to taste
- Optional toppings: avocado, cilantro, sour cream

Instructions
1. Preheat your Instant Vortex Plus Versa Zone air fryer to (190°C).
2. Brush both sides of the corn tortillas with vegetable oil and sprinkle with salt.
3. Place the tortillas in the air fryer basket and cook for 3-4 minutes, or until crispy.
4. While the tortillas are cooking, heat the black beans in a saucepan over medium heat.
5. Once the tortillas are done, remove them from the Instant Vortex Plus Versa Zone basket and place them on a plate.
6. Spoon the heated black beans over the tortillas.
7. Crack the eggs directly over the black beans and season with salt and pepper.
8. Spoon the salsa over the eggs and sprinkle with shredded cheddar cheese.
9. Place the plate back in the air fryer basket and cook for 6-7 minutes, or until the eggs are cooked to your liking and the cheese is melted.
10. Once done, remove the plate from the Instant Vortex Plus Versa Zone and let it cool for a few minutes.
11. Serve the Huevos Rancheros with any desired toppings, such as avocado, cilantro, or sour cream

Crispy, cinnamon-sugar doughnuts

Serves: 4
Prep time: 10 minutes
Cook time: 10 minutes

Ingredients:
- 125ml of water
- 46g of unsalted butter
- 12g of granulated sugar
- 1g of salt
- 125g of all-purpose flour
- 2 eggs
- 12ml of vanilla extract
- 50g of granulated sugar, for coating
- 2g of ground cinnamon, for coating

Instructions
1. Preheat your Instant Vortex Plus Versa Zone air fryer to 190°C.
2. In a medium saucepan, combine the water, unsalted butter, 1 tbsp of granulated sugar, and salt. Heat over medium heat until the butter is melted and the mixture is simmering.
3. Remove the saucepan from the heat and add the all-purpose flour. Stir until the mixture forms a smooth dough.
4. Add the eggs, one at a time, stirring vigorously after each addition. The dough should become smooth and glossy.
5. Stir in the vanilla extract.
6. Transfer the dough to a piping bag fitted with a star tip.
7. Pipe the dough into long, thin strips directly into the Instant Vortex Plus Versa Zone

basket.
8. Cook the churros for 7-8 minutes, or until they are golden brown and crispy.
9. While the churros are cooking, mix together the remaining 1/4 cup of granulated sugar and 1 tsp of ground cinnamon in a shallow dish.
10. Once the churros are done, remove them from the air fryer basket and immediately toss them in the cinnamon sugar mixture to coat.

Divorced eggs with bold flavors

Serves: 2
Prep time: 10 minutes
Cook time: 10 minutes

Ingredients:
- 4 corn tortillas
- 60g of crumbled queso fresco or feta cheese
- 15ml of olive oil
- 1/2 onion, chopped
- 2 garlic cloves, minced
- 400g of diced tomatoes
- 60ml of water
- Salt and pepper, to taste
- 30ml of vegetable oil
- 4 eggs
- Optional toppings: chopped cilantro, sliced avocado, hot sauce

Instructions
1. Preheat your Instant Vortex Plus Versa Zone air fryer to 190°C.
2. Place the corn tortillas in the air fryer basket and cook for 5-7 minutes, or until crispy.
3. Remove the tortillas from the Instant Vortex Plus Versa Zone and set aside.
4. In a skillet over medium heat, heat the olive oil.
5. Add the chopped onion and garlic to the skillet and cook for 5-7 minutes, or until softened.
6. Pour the can of diced tomatoes and water into the skillet and stir to combine.
7. Season the mixture with salt and pepper to taste.
8. Once the mixture is heated through, transfer it to a baking dish that fits into the Instant Voertex Plus Versa Zone basket.
9. Use a spoon to divide the tomato mixture in half and push each half to the opposite ends of the baking dish to create two separate "sauce" sections.
10. In a separate skillet, heat the vegetable oil over medium heat.
11. Crack two eggs into the skillet and cook to your desired level of doneness.
12. Repeat with the remaining two eggs. Place two crispy tortillas on each plate.
13. Spoon one egg onto each tortilla, placing one egg in each "sauce" section. Sprinkle crumbled queso fresco or feta cheese over the eggs and sauces

Savory, flaky pastry filled with goodness

Serves: 4-6
Prep time: 20 minutes
Cook time: 25-30 minutes

Ingredients:
- 1 pre-made pie crust (9 inch
- 23 cm)
- 4 large eggs
- 200 ml of heavy cream
- 200 ml of milk
- 100 g of grated Gruyere cheese
- 1/2 tsp of salt
- 1/4 tsp of black pepper
- 1/4 tsp of ground nutmeg
- Optional fillings: cooked and chopped bacon,

diced ham, sautéed mushrooms, chopped spinach, caramelized onions, etc

Instructions:
1. Preheat your Instant Vortex Plus Versa Zone air fryer to 160°C
2. Place the pre-made pie crust into a 9 inch (23 cm) pie dish.
3. In a large mixing bowl, whisk together the eggs, heavy cream, milk, salt, black pepper, and ground nutmeg.
4. Add the grated Gruyere cheese to the mixing bowl and stir to combine.
5. If using any optional fillings, spread them evenly across the bottom of the pie crust.
6. Pour the egg and cheese mixture over the optional fillings, filling the pie crust almost to the top.
7. Carefully place the filled pie dish into the Instant Vortex Plus Versa Zone basket.
8. Air fry the quiche for 25-30 minutes, or until the filling is set and the top is golden brown.
9. Remove the quiche from the Instant Vortex Plus Versa Zone and allow it to cool for a few minutes before slicing and serving.

Flavorful, handheld Latin American pies

Serves: 4-6
Prep time: 30 minutes
Cook time: 15-20 minutes

Ingredients:
- 240g of all-purpose flour
- 1/4 tsp of salt
- 56g cup of unsalted butter, chilled and cubed
- 60ml of cold water
- 1 large egg, lightly beaten
- 115g of cooked and seasoned ground beef or chicken
- 56g shredded cheese

Optional fillings:
- sautéed onions, cooked vegetables, etc.
- 1 egg yolk, beaten with 1 tbsp of water

Instructions:
1. In a large mixing bowl, whisk together the flour and salt.
2. Using a pastry blender or your fingers, cut in the chilled butter until the mixture resembles coarse crumbs.
3. Add the cold water and lightly beaten egg to the mixing bowl, and stir until a dough forms.
4. Knead the dough on a floured surface for a few minutes, then wrap it in plastic wrap and refrigerate for at least 30 minutes.
5. Preheat your Instant Vortex Plus Versa Zone air fryer to 190°C
6. Roll out the chilled dough on a floured surface until it's about 1 8 inch (3 mm) thick.
7. Use a round cookie cutter or a large glass to cut circles out of the dough.
8. Place a small amount of the cooked and seasoned ground beef or chicken, shredded cheese, and any optional fillings onto each circle of dough.
9. Fold the dough over the filling to form a half-moon shape, then press the edges together to seal.
10. Brush the beaten egg yolk and water mixture over the top of each empanada.
11. Place the empanadas in a single layer in the Instant Vortex Plus Versa Zone fryer basket, and air fry them for 15-20 minutes, or until the crust is golden brown and crispy.
12. Serve the empanadas hot with your favorite dipping sauce

CHAPTER 2 : LUNCH

Grandma's Potato Gratin

Prep time: 10 minutes
Cook time: 25 minutes
Serves 5

Ingredients

- 1 tbsp butter, melted
- 900g Maris Piper potatoes, peeled and sliced
- 250ml full-fat milk
- 260ml double cream
- 1 garlic clove, peeled and halved
- 1/2 tsp dried basil
- 1 sprig of rosemary, chopped
- 1 sprig of thyme, chopped
- 1/2 tsp red pepper flakes, crushed
- Sea salt and ground black pepper, to taste.
- 1 small onion, chopped
- 20g Parmesan cheese, freshly grated

Instructions

1. Rub the melted butter all over the interior of a gratin dish. Then, pat dry potato slices with a tea towel.
2. In a medium saucepan, bring the milk and cream to a rolling boil. Add the garlic and herbs; remove the saucepan from the heat. Sprinkle in red pepper flakes, salt, and pepper; set aside and keep warm.
3. Layer half the potato slices and chopped onion in the prepared dish, adding salt and black pepper to taste.
4. Pour half of the cream mixture over the potatoes, then add the rest of the potato slices and onion. Pour over the rest of the cream mixture. Scatter Parmesan cheese (preferably freshly grated) over the top
5. Select "Bake" and set the time for 25 minutes and the temperature to 170 degrees C.
6. When the display shows "Turn Food", remove the cooking basket and rotate your gratin dish to ensure even cooking. Insert the basket again to continue cooking until the top is golden and bubbly. Devour!

The Easiest British Fish Pie Ever

Prep time: 10 minutes
Cook time: 38 minutes
Serves 5

Ingredients

- 900g Maris Piper potatoes, peeled and halved
- 2 tbsp butter
- 350ml plain milk
- 20g oat flour (plain flour works well too)
- 1 small shallot, chopped
- 1 garlic clove, minced
- 1 (320g) pack fish pie mix (skinless fish)
- 1 tbsp fresh parsley, finely chopped
- A pinch of grated nutmeg
- 1/2 tsp chilli flakes (optional)
- Sea salt and ground black pepper, to taste
- A handful of grated cheddar

Instructions

1. Add your potatoes to the Air Fryer cooking tray. Select "Air Fry", and set the temperature to 190 degrees C and the time to 20 minutes.
2. Meanwhile, rub 1 tablespoon of the melted butter all over the interior of an ovenproof baking dish. Set it aside.
3. Cook the remaining 1 tablespoon of butter, flour, shallots, and garlic in another saucepan for about 2 minutes, until fragrant. Gradually whisk in 300ml of milk and bring to a rapid boil. Whisk constantly to avoid sticking at the bottom of the saucepan. Cook until the

sauce has thickened.
4. Fold in the fish and add the herbs and spices. Spoon the mixture into the prepared baking dish.
5. Mash the potatoes with the remaining 50ml of milk. Spoon the mashed potatoes on top of the pie; sprinkle with grated cheddar cheese.
6. Select "Bake" and set the time for 18 minutes and the temperature to 170 degrees C.
7. When the display shows "Turn Food", remove the cooking basket and rotate the baking dish to ensure even cooking. Insert the basket again to continue cooking. Bon appétit!

Scottish Rumbledethumps

Prep time: 10 minutes
Cook time: 35 minutes
Serves 6

Ingredients
- 1kg Maris Piper or King Edward potatoes, peeled and diced
- 1 head of green cabbage, shredded
- 2 shallots, sliced
- 2 tbsp butter
- 4 tbsp plain milk
- 100g cheddar cheese, shredded
- Sea salt and ground black pepper, to taste

Instructions
1. Arrange potatoes in the Air Fryer cooking tray. Select "Air Fry", and set the temperature to 190 degrees C and the time to 20 minutes.
2. Mash potatoes with 1 tablespoon of butter. Thoroughly combine the potatoes with the other Ingredients and spoon the mixture into a lightly greased gratin dish; smooth the top with a spatula.
3. Select "Bake" and set the time for 15 minutes and the temperature to 170 degrees C.
4. When the display shows "Turn Food", remove the cooking basket and rotate the gratin dish to ensure even cooking. Insert the basket again to continue cooking.
5. Good serving options include sausages, refried beans, or roast. Bon appétit!

Traditional Beef Wellington

Prep time: 10 minutes
Cook time: 30 minutes
Serves 6

Ingredients
- 2 tbsp butter
- 250g brown mushrooms, chopped
- 1 medium carrot, grated
- 1 onion, finely chopped
- 700g beef mince
- 100g tomato ketchup
- 1 large garlic clove, finely chopped
- 2 medium eggs
- 1/2 tsp cayenne pepper
- Sea salt and ground black pepper, to taste
- 1 tbsp coriander, chopped
- 250g pack puff pastry

Instructions
1. Melt 1 tablespoon of the butter in a frying pan over a medium-high flame. Sauté the mushrooms, carrot, and onion for about 3 minutes, until they are fragrant and tender.
2. In a mixing bowl, combine the beef mince, tomato ketchup, garlic, 1 egg, cayenne pepper, salt, black pepper, and coriander.
3. Press the mixture into a lightly-greased baking tray. Select "Roast" and set the time for 15 minutes and the temperature to 180 degrees C.
4. Meanwhile, beat the remaining egg with a little water.
5. Roll puff pastry into a rectangle. Spread the sauteed vegetable mixture along the middle of the rectangle. Place the prepared meatloaf on top and bring the edges together; brush

with the egg wash.
6. Rub the remaining 1 tablespoon of the butter all over the interior of the baking tray.
7. Place your Beef Wellington on the baking tray. Select "Bake" and set the time for 15 minutes and the temperature to 175 degrees C.
8. Bon appétit!

Traditional Christmas Turkey

Prep time: 10 minutes
Cook time: 50 minutes
Serves 6

Ingredients

- 1 small (3-3.5kg) turkey, bone-in
- Sea salt and ground black pepper, to taste
- 100g butter
- 200g pancetta
- 2 large shallots, quartered
- 4 carrots, halved
- 2 celery sticks, halved
- 6 garlic cloves, peeled
- 1 tbsp fresh sage, chopped
- 2 tbsp fresh parsley, chopped
- 2 bay leaves

Instructions

1. Season the turkey with salt and pepper and lower it on a roasting tray; now, spread butter over the entire surface and cover it with pancetta
2. Arrange the other Ingredients around the turkey. Then pour 1 litre of water into the roasting tray and cover everything with tin foil.
3. Select "Roast" and set the time for 50 minutes and the temperature to 200 degrees C.
4. If the turkey has reached 75 degrees C, it's done. Enjoy!

Roast Rib of Beef

Prep time: 10 minutes + marinating time
Cook time: 20 minutes
Serves 6

Ingredients

Marinade:
- 1 tbsp toasted cumin seeds
- 2 tbsp garlic powder
- 1 tbsp cracked black pepper
- 2 tbsp olive oil
- 2 tbsp smoked paprika
- 100g ketchup
- 50g English mustard
- 50g brown sauce

Roast Rib of Beef:
- 2 kg meaty beef ribs
- 2 shallots, sliced

Instructions

1. In a glass or ceramic bowl, whisk all Ingredients for the marinade.
2. Use a knife to make a deep hole in each rib, and add them to the marinade. Let the ribs marinate for a couple of hours in your refrigerator.
3. Add beef ribs and shallots to a lightly greased baking tray.
4. To make the sauce, simmer the marinade Ingredients until the mixture becomes rich and glossy. Spoon 1/2 of the sauce over the beef ribs
5. Select "Roast" and set the time for 20 minutes and the temperature to 200 degrees C.
6. When the display shows "Turn Food", spoon the remaining sauce over the beef ribs.
7. If the ribs have reached 96 degrees C, they're done. Enjoy!

Baked Glazed Ham

Prep time: 10 minutes
Cook time: 20 minutes
Serves 6

Ingredients

- 2kg fully cooked ham, boneless

- 1 sprig thyme
- 2 bay leaves
- 1 tbsp fried sage
- 1 onion, halved
- 2 carrots, roughly chopped
- Sea salt and black peppercorns, to taste

Glaze:
- 60g honey
- 20ml freshly squeezed orange juice
- 1 tbsp English mustard

Instructions

1. Add cooked ham, herbs, and vegetables to a lightly greased baking tray. Add salt and black peppercorns; cover it with tin foil.
2. Select "Roast" and set the time for 50 minutes and the temperature to 175 degrees C.
3. When the display shows "Turn Food", spoon the glaze over the top of your ham. Insert the basket again to continue cooking.
4. When your ham reached 60 degrees C, it's done. Allow it to rest for at least 10 minutes before carving and serving. Enjoy!

Roast Pork with Crackling

Prep time: 10 minutes + marinating time
Cook time: 18 minutes
Serves 5

Ingredients

- 1kg pork loin with the skin scored, rolled and tied
- 1 tbsp sea salt
- 5 garlic cloves, sliced into thin slivers
- 1 sprig thyme, leaves picked
- 1 sprig rosemary, leaves picked

Instructions

1. Rub salt in the pork skin. Leave it for about 2 hours in your fridge.
2. Then, turn the pork rind-side down and create 8- 9 deep incisions along the meat using a small knife.
3. Poke a sliver of garlic and a few leaves of herbs in each incision. Now, turn the meat the right way up and lower it into the Air Fryer cooking tray.
4. Select "Roast" and set the time for 18 minutes and the temperature to 190 degrees C.
5. When the display shows "Turn Food", turn it over. Insert the basket again to continue cooking.
6. When the pork reached 68 degrees C, it's done. Leave it for about 10 minutes before carving and serving. Enjoy!

Fish in Ginger-Shallot Sauce

Prep time: 10 minutes
Cook time: 12 minutes
Serves 4

Ingredients

- 400g white fish fillet
- Sea salt and ground black pepper, to taste
- 1 tsp olive oil

Batter:
- 1 egg
- 100g corn flour
- 1 tsp garlic powder
- 1 tsp dried oregano

Sauce:
- 1 small shallot, peeled and sliced
- 1 tbsp soy sauce (or tamari sauce)
- 1 tsp honey
- 100ml vegetable stock
- 2 tbsp dry white wine
- 1 thumb-sized piece of ginger, minced

Instructions

1. Toss the fish fillets with salt, pepper, and olive oil.
2. Whisk the egg in a shallow bowl; combine corn flour with garlic powder and oregano in a separate shallow bowl (or a plate).
3. Dip the fish fillets in the egg, and then, coat

them with the flour mixture.
4. Select "Air Fry" and set the time for 10 minutes and the temperature to 200 degrees C.
5. When the display shows "Turn Food", turn the fillets over. Insert the basket again to continue cooking.
6. Meanwhile, whisk the sauce Ingredients in a bowl. Get a saucepan or wok up to high heat on the hob and bring the sauce to a rolling boil. Immediately turn to a simmer and let it cook for 10 to 12 minutes, until the sauce has thickened.
7. When your Instant Vortex Plus Air Fryer finishes, toss the fish fillets with warm sauce and serve immediately. Enjoy!

Bangers and Mash

Prep time: 10 minutes
Cook time: 12 minutes
Serves 5

Ingredients
- 5 pork smoked sausages
- 1 tsp olive oil

Mash:
- 900g floury potatoes such as King Edward, peeled and diced into 2.5 cm chunks
- 90ml whole milk
- 20g butter
- A pinch of grated nutmeg
- Sea salt and ground black pepper, to taste

Instructions
1. Slide the tray divider into the cooking tray. Put the cooking basket into the Air Fryer and then, press the Control Dial two times quickly to activate Dual Zone cooking.
2. Toss sausages with olive oil and lower them into Drawer 1 of your Air Fryer. Select "Air Fry" on this drawer and set the temperature to 190 degrees C and the time to 10 minutes.
3. Place the potatoes in Drawer 2. Select "Air Fry", and set the temperature to 200 degrees C and the time to 12 minutes. Select "SyncFinish" to ensure both drawers finish at the same time.
4. When the display shows "Turn Food", remove the cooking basket and carefully flip your food. Insert the basket again to continue cooking.
5. Mash the potatoes with the milk, butter, and nutmeg; add salt and pepper to taste.
6. Bon appétit!

Vegetarian Cottage Pie

Prep time: 10 minutes
Cook time: 27 minutes
Serves 5

Ingredients
- 1 tbsp olive oil
- 1 onion, chopped
- 1 small bell pepper, sliced
- 1 head of celery, chopped
- 200g chestnut mushrooms, sliced
- 2 garlic cloves, finely chopped
- 1 tsp dried rosemary
- 1 tsp dried sage
- 200g tofu, chopped
- 200ml vegetable stock
- 4 tbsp tomato purée

Topping:
- 1kg King Edwards potatoes, peeled and diced into 2.5 cm chunks
- 20g butter
- 50ml milk
- Sea salt and ground black pepper, to taste
- 50g cheddar cheese, grated

Instructions
1. Heat olive oil in a large saucepan over medium-high heat. Once hot, saute the onion, pepper, and celery for about 3 minutes until they've softened.
2. Add the mushrooms, garlic, herbs, tofu,

stock, and tomato purée and stir to combine; continue simmering, partially covered, for about 10 minutes or until the sauce has thickened slightly.
3. In the meantime, add potatoes to the Air Fryer cooking basket. Select "Air Fry" and set the time for 12 minutes and the temperature to 200 degrees C.
4. When the display shows "Turn Food", shake the basket. Insert the basket again to continue cooking.
5. Mash the potatoes with the butter and milk; salt and pepper to taste. Spoon the tofu mixture into a lightly-greased oven-proof baking dish, then top with mash.
6. Select "Bake" and set the time for 15 minutes and the temperature to 180 degrees C.
7. When the display shows "Turn Food", remove the cooking basket and rotate the baking dish to ensure even cooking. Scatter cheddar cheese over the top. Insert the basket again to continue cooking.
8. Bon appétit!

Caprese Panini Recipe

Serves: 2
Prep time: 10 minutes
Cook time: 5-7 minutes

Ingredients:
- 4 slices of crusty bread
- 4-6 fresh basil leaves
- 1 medium-sized tomato, sliced
- 200g fresh mozzarella cheese, sliced
- 2 tbsp balsamic glaze
- 2 tbsp olive oil

Instructions
1. Preheat your Instant Vortex Plus Versa Zone to 375°F (190°C).
2. Brush one side of each bread slice with olive oil.
3. On the non-oiled side of 2 slices of bread, layer the mozzarella cheese, tomato slices, and basil leaves.
4. Drizzle balsamic glaze over the Ingredients.
5. Top each sandwich with the remaining slices of bread (oiled side facing outwards).
6. Place the sandwiches in the Instant Vortex Plus Versa Zone and cook for 5-7 minutes, or until the cheese is melted and the bread is golden brown.
7. Once cooked, remove the sandwiches from the Instant Vortex Plus Versa Zone and let them cool for a minute before slicing them in half and serving.
8. Enjoy your delicious Caprese Panini!

Mushroom Risotto

Serves: 4
Prep time: 10 minutes
Cook time: 25 minutes

Ingredients:
- 1 liter chicken or vegetable broth
- 2 tbsp olive oil
- 1 medium onion, diced
- 2 garlic cloves, minced
- 250g mushrooms, sliced
- 300g Arborio rice
- 100ml dry white wine
- 50g grated Parmesan cheese
- Salt and pepper, to taste

Instructions
1. Preheat your Instant Vortex Plus Versa Zone to 180°C
2. In a saucepan, heat the broth and keep it warm on low heat.
3. In a separate large saucepan or Dutch oven, heat the olive oil over medium heat.
4. Add the onion and garlic, and cook until the onion is translucent.
5. Add the sliced mushrooms and cook for about 5 minutes, until the mushrooms are

tender and browned.
6. Add the Arborio rice and stir until each grain is coated in oil.
7. Pour in the white wine and stir until the liquid has been absorbed.
8. Begin adding the warm broth, one ladle at a time, stirring constantly and waiting for the liquid to be absorbed before adding more.
9. Continue this process until the rice is cooked through and has a creamy consistency, which should take about 20-25 minutes.
10. Stir in the grated Parmesan cheese, salt and pepper to taste.
11. Once fully cooked, remove the saucepan from heat and let it rest for a few minutes before serving.Enjoy your delicious Mushroom Risotto!

Italian Wedding Soup

Serves: 6
Prep time: 20 minutes
Cook time: 30 minutes

Ingredients:
- 450g ground beef
- 60g breadcrumbs
- 25g grated Parmesan cheese
- 2 garlic cloves, minced
- 1 egg, beaten
- Salt and pepper, to taste
- 15ml olive oil
- 1 medium onion, diced
- 2 celery stalks, diced
- 2 carrots, diced
- 1.5 liters chicken broth
- 200g baby spinach, chopped
- 150g Acini di Pepe pasta

Instructions
1. Preheat your Instant Vortex Plus Versa Zone to 190°C
2. In a mixing bowl, combine the ground beef, breadcrumbs, Parmesan cheese, garlic, egg, salt and pepper. Mix well to combine.
3. Roll the mixture into small meatballs, about 2.5cm in diameter.
4. In a large saucepan or Dutch oven, heat the olive oil over medium heat.
5. Add the onion, celery, and carrot, and cook until the vegetables are tender.
6. Add the chicken broth and bring to a boil.
7. Add the meatballs and Acini di Pepe pasta, and reduce heat to a simmer. Cook for about 10 minutes, or until the meatballs are cooked through and the pasta is tender.
8. Stir in the chopped baby spinach and let it wilt for a couple of minutes.
9. Once fully cooked, remove the saucepan from heat and let it rest for a few minutes before serving.Enjoy your delicious Italian Wedding Soup!

Mediterranean Veggie Wrap

Serves: 4
Prep time: 20 minutes
Cook time: 5-7 minutes

Ingredients:
- 4 large whole wheat wraps
- 120g hummus
- 60g baby spinach leaves
- 80g chopped sun-dried tomatoes
- 70g crumbled feta cheese
- 40g thinly sliced red onion
- 40g sliced Kalamata olives
- 30ml olive oil
- 15ml lemon juice
- 1 clove garlic, minced
- Salt and pepper, to taste

Instructions
1. Preheat your Instant Vortex Plus Versa Zone to 190°C
2. In a small mixing bowl, whisk together the

olive oil, lemon juice, garlic, salt and pepper to create a dressing.
3. Lay out each wrap on a clean surface and spread about 2 tablespoons (30g) of hummus in the center of each wrap.
4. Add a handful (about 15g) of baby spinach leaves on top of the hummus, followed by the sun-dried tomatoes (about 20g), feta cheese (about 18g), red onion (about 10g) and Kalamata olives (about 10g).
5. Drizzle the dressing over the veggies.
6. Roll up the wraps tightly, tucking in the sides as you go.
7. Place the wraps in the Instant Vortex Plus Versa Zone and cook for 5-7 minutes, or until the wraps are slightly crispy on the outside and the filling is heated through.
8. Once fully cooked, remove the wraps from the Versa Zone and let them cool for a couple of minutes before serving

Chicken Caesar Wrap

Serves: 4
Prep time: 20 minutes
Cook time: 5-7 minutes

Ingredients:
- 4 large whole wheat wraps
- 160g chopped romaine lettuce
- 400g cooked chicken breast, sliced
- 120g Caesar dressing
- 50g grated Parmesan cheese
- 40g chopped red onion
- 40g chopped cherry tomatoes
- 2 tablespoons (30ml) lemon juice
- 2 cloves garlic, minced
- Salt and pepper, to taste

Instructions
1. Preheat your Instant Vortex Plus Versa Zone to 190°C
2. In a small mixing bowl, whisk together the Caesar dressing, lemon juice, garlic, salt, and pepper to create a dressing.
3. Lay out each wrap on a clean surface and spread about 2 tablespoons (30g) of the dressing in the center of each wrap.
4. Add a handful (about 40g) of chopped romaine lettuce on top of the dressing, followed by the sliced chicken breast (about 100g), grated Parmesan cheese (about 25g), chopped red onion (about 10g), and chopped cherry tomatoes (about 10g).
5. Drizzle the remaining dressing over the chicken and veggies.
6. Roll up the wraps tightly, tucking in the sides as you go.
7. Place the wraps in the Instant Vortex Plus Versa Zone and cook for 5-7 minutes, or until the wraps are slightly crispy on the outside and the filling is heated through.
8. Once fully cooked, remove the wraps from the Versa Zone and let them cool for a couple of minutes before serving

Buffalo Cauliflower Bites

Serves: 4-6
Prep time: 15 minutes
Cook Time: 25 minutes

Ingredients:
- 1 large head of cauliflower, cut into bite-size florets
- 60g of All-purpose flour
- 120ml cup water
- 2g teaspoon garlic powder
- 2g teaspoon onion powder
- 1g teaspoon salt
- 1g teaspoon black pepper
- 120ml cup of hot sauce
- 60g cup unsalted butter, melted

Instructions
1. Preheat the Instant Vortex Plus Versa Zone to

205°C
2. In a large mixing bowl, whisk together the flour, water, garlic powder, onion powder, salt, and black pepper until a smooth batter forms.
3. Add the cauliflower florets to the batter and toss until each piece is well coated.
4. Line the instant Vortex Plus Versa Zone fryer basket with parchment paper and arrange the cauliflower in a single layer.
5. Air fry the cauliflower at 205°C for 20-25 minutes, flipping halfway through, or until golden brown and crispy.
6. While the cauliflower is cooking, in a small bowl, whisk together the hot sauce and melted butter until well combined.
7. Once the cauliflower is done, transfer it to a large mixing bowl and pour the buffalo sauce over the top. Toss the cauliflower until each piece is well coated.
8. Serve the buffalo cauliflower bites hot, garnished with sliced green onions and a side of ranch or blue cheese dressing, if desired. Enjoy

Greek Turkey Burgers

Serves: 4
Prep time: 15 minutes
Cook Time: 15 minutes

Ingredients:
- 450g of ground turkey
- 40g of feta cheese, crumbled
- 40g of red onion, finely chopped
- 10g of cup fresh parsley, chopped
- 2 cloves garlic, minced
- 2g of dried oregano
- 2g of teaspoon salt
- 1g of teaspoon black pepper
- 4 hamburger buns
- Tzatziki sauce, for serving
- Sliced tomato, for serving
- Sliced red onion, for serving
- Lettuce leaves, for serving

Instructions
1. Preheat the Instant Vortex Plus Versa Zone to 190°C.
2. In a large mixing bowl, combine the ground turkey, feta cheese, chopped red onion, parsley, minced garlic, dried oregano, salt, and black pepper. Use your hands to mix everything together until well combined.
3. Divide the mixture into 4 equal portions and shape each portion into a patty, about 1/2-inch thick.
4. Place the patties in the Instant Vortex Plus Versa Zone air fryer basket and cook at (190°C) for 15 minutes, flipping halfway through, or until the internal temperature reaches (75°C).
5. While the burgers are cooking, prepare the toppings and warm the hamburger buns.
6. Once the burgers are done, assemble the burgers by placing each patty on a bun, topped with a dollop of tzatziki sauce, sliced tomato, sliced red onion, and lettuce leaves.
7. Serve the Greek turkey burgers

Ratatouille

Serves: 4
Prep time: 20 minutes
Cook Time: 30 minutes

Ingredients:
- 1 medium eggplant, diced into 1-inch pieces (450g)
- 2 medium zucchinis, diced into 1-inch pieces (300g)
- 1 red bell pepper, diced into 1-inch pieces (150g)
- 1 yellow bell pepper, diced into 1-inch pieces (150g)
- 1 large onion, diced (200g)

- 3 cloves garlic, minced
- 1 can diced tomatoes (400g)
- 2 tablespoons tomato paste (30ml)
- 1 tablespoon balsamic vinegar (15ml)
- 1 teaspoon dried thyme (2g)
- 1/2 teaspoon dried oregano (1g)
- Salt and pepper, to taste
- 2 tablespoons olive oil (30ml)
- Fresh basil leaves, chopped (optional)

Instructions

1. Preheat the Instant Vortex Plus Versa Zone to (190°C).
2. In a large mixing bowl, combine the diced eggplant, zucchini, red and yellow bell peppers, diced onion, minced garlic, diced tomatoes (including the juice), tomato paste, balsamic vinegar, dried thyme, dried oregano, salt, pepper, and olive oil. Stir until everything is evenly coated.
3. Transfer the mixture to the Instant Vortex Plus Versa Zone air fryer basket, spreading it out evenly in a single layer.
4. Cook at (190°C) for 30 minutes, stirring halfway through, or until the vegetables are tender and lightly browned.
5. Once the ratatouille is done, transfer it to a serving dish and sprinkle with chopped fresh basil leaves, if desired.
6. Serve the ratatouille hot or cold as a side dish or as a main course with crusty bread or pasta, if desired. Enjoy!

Pesto Pasta Salad

Serves: 4-6
Prep time: 10 minutes
Cook time: 10 minutes

Ingredients:

- 500g fusilli pasta
- 100g sun-dried tomatoes, chopped
- 100g black olives, sliced
- 50g pine nuts
- 2 cloves garlic, minced
- 100g parmesan cheese, grated
- 1 bunch fresh basil leaves
- olive oil
- 2 tbsp lemon juice
- Salt and pepper to taste

Instructions

1. Cook the fusilli pasta in a pot of boiling salted water until it is al dente, following the Instructions on the package. Drain the pasta and set it aside to cool.
2. While the pasta is cooking, prepare the pesto sauce. In a food processor, blend together the garlic, parmesan cheese, basil leaves, pine nuts, olive oil, and lemon juice until the mixture is smooth and creamy.
3. In a large bowl, mix the cooked pasta, sun-dried tomatoes, black olives, and pesto sauce until everything is well combined.
4. Season the pasta salad with salt and pepper to taste. Cover the bowl with plastic wrap and refrigerate for at least 30 minutes to allow the flavors to meld.
5. Serve the pesto pasta salad chilled, garnished with additional parmesan cheese and fresh basil leaves, if desired. Enjoy

Vegan Buddha Bowl

Serves: 4
Prep time: 10 minutes
Cook Time: 20 minutes

Ingredients:

- Quinoaa (360g)
- 1 can of chickpeas, drained and rinsed (240g)
- 2 medium sweet potatoes, peeled and diced (600g)
- 1 red onion, sliced (150g)
- 2 tbsp of olive oil (30ml)
- 1 tsp of ground cumin (2g)

- 1 tsp of smoked paprika (2g)
- Salt and pepper to taste
- mixed greens (120g)
- 1 avocado, sliced (200g)
- cherry tomatoes, halved (150g)
- Tahini (60ml) *use olive oil if you can't get tahini*
- lemon juice (60ml)
- water (60ml)
- 2 cloves of garlic, minced (6g)

Instructions

1. Preheat your Instant Vortex Plus Versa Zone to (200°C).
2. In a large bowl, combine the diced sweet potatoes, sliced onion, olive oil, cumin, smoked paprika, salt, and pepper. Toss until the vegetables are evenly coated.
3. Arrange the seasoned vegetables on the Instant Vortex Plus Versa Zone basket in a single layer. Cook for 20 minutes or until the vegetables are tender and golden brown.
4. While the vegetables are cooking, rinse the quinoa and cook according to the package Instructions. Set aside.
5. In a small bowl, whisk together the tahini, lemon juice, water, and minced garlic to make the dressing. Set aside.
6. Once the vegetables are done, assemble the Buddha bowls. Divide the cooked quinoa, mixed greens, roasted sweet potatoes, and chickpeas among four bowls.
7. Drizzle the tahini dressing over each bowl and top with sliced avocado and cherry tomatoes.

Tomato and Mozzarella Panini Recipe

Serves: 2
Prep time: 10 minutes
Cook time: 10 minutes

Ingredients:

- 4 slices of bread (wholemeal or sourdough)
- 2 medium-sized tomatoes, sliced
- 150g fresh mozzarella, sliced
- 2 tbsp pesto sauce
- 1 tbsp olive oil

Instructions

1. Preheat your Instant Vortex Plus Versa Zone on the Panini setting.
2. Spread 1 tablespoon of pesto sauce on each slice of bread.
3. Layer the sliced tomatoes and fresh mozzarella on two slices of bread and top with the remaining slices of bread.
4. Brush the top and bottom of each sandwich with olive oil.
5. Place the sandwiches in the Instant Vortex Plus Versa Zone and cook for 5-7 minutes, or until the bread is golden brown and the cheese is melted.
6. Serve hot.

Pheasant Pie Recipe

Serves: 6
Prep time: 30 minutes
Cook time: 2 hours

Ingredients:

- 1 pheasant (approx. 700g), deboned and diced
- 1 onion, diced
- 2 garlic cloves, minced
- 2 medium-sized carrots, peeled and diced
- 2 celery stalks, diced
- 2 tbsp olive oil
- 2 tbsp plain flour
- 500ml chicken or vegetable stock
- 150ml red wine
- 2 sprigs of thyme
- 1 bay leaf
- Salt and pepper, to taste
- 500g puff pastry

- 1 egg, beaten

Instructions

1. Preheat your Instant Vortex Plus Versa Zone on the Bake setting to 200°C.
2. Heat the olive oil in a large saucepan over medium heat.
3. Add the onion, garlic, carrots, and celery, and cook for 5 minutes, or until softened.
4. Add the diced pheasant and cook for another 5 minutes, or until browned.
5. Sprinkle the flour over the mixture and stir well to combine.
6. Gradually add the chicken or vegetable stock and red wine, stirring constantly to avoid lumps.
7. Add the thyme and bay leaf, and season with salt and pepper.
8. Simmer the mixture for 15-20 minutes, or until the sauce has thickened and the vegetables and pheasant are tender.
9. Remove the thyme sprigs and bay leaf.
10. Roll out the puff pastry on a lightly floured surface and cut into a shape that will fit over the top of your pie dish.
11. Transfer the pheasant mixture to a pie dish and cover with the puff pastry, trimming any excess pastry from the edges.
12. Brush the pastry with the beaten egg.
13. Place the pie dish in the Instant Vortex Plus Versa Zone and bake for 30-40 minutes, or until the pastry is golden brown and crispy. Serve

Chorizo and Red Pepper Tart Recipe

Serves: 6
Prep time: 20 minutes
Cook time: 45 minutes

Ingredients:
- 1 sheet of ready-rolled puff pastry (320g)
- 2 red bell peppers, deseeded and sliced
- 1 chorizo sausage, sliced
- 1 onion, chopped
- 1 garlic clove, minced
- 3 eggs
- 200ml double cream
- 100g grated cheddar cheese
- Salt and pepper, to taste
- 1 tbsp olive oil

Instructions

1. Preheat your Instant Vortex Plus Versa Zone on the Bake setting to 200°C.
2. Roll out the puff pastry and line a tart tin with it, trimming any excess pastry from the edges.
3. Prick the pastry base with a fork and bake in the Instant Vortex Plus Versa Zone for 10 minutes.
4. In a frying pan, heat the olive oil and cook the chorizo, onion, and garlic over medium heat for 5-7 minutes, or until the onion is soft and the chorizo is browned.
5. Add the sliced red peppers and continue cooking for a further 5 minutes.
6. In a bowl, whisk together the eggs and double cream.
7. Season the egg mixture with salt and pepper.
8. Spread the chorizo and pepper mixture over the pastry base and sprinkle with grated cheddar cheese.
9. Pour the egg mixture over the top and bake in the Instant Vortex Plus Versa Zone for 25-30 minutes, or until the filling is set and the top is golden brown.

Scottish Scallops

Serves: 2
Prep time: 10 minutes
Cook time: 5 minutes

Ingredients:
- 8 fresh Scottish scallops (250 g)

- 2 tablespoons olive oil (30 ml)
- 1 tablespoon unsalted butter (15 g)
- Salt and pepper to taste

Instructions

1. Rinse the scallops under cold water and pat them dry with a paper towel.
2. Season the scallops with salt and pepper on both sides.
3. Place the olive oil and butter in the instant vortex plus versa zone and select the 'air fry' function to 180°c.
4. Once the oil is hot, place the scallops in the basket and cook for 2-3 minutes on each side, until golden brown.
5. Serve immediately.

Cullen Skink Recipe

Serves: 4
Prep time: 15 minutes
Cook time: 45 minutes

Ingredients:

- 450 g smoked haddock fillets
- 1 liter whole milk
- 1 onion, finely chopped
- 2 medium-sized potatoes, peeled and diced
- 2 tablespoons unsalted butter
- 100 ml heavy cream
- Salt and pepper to taste
- Chopped fresh parsley, to serve

Instructions

1. Preheat the Instant Vortex Plus Versa Zone to 180°C.
2. In a large pot, combine the smoked haddock fillets and milk. Bring to a simmer over medium heat and cook for 10 minutes, or until the fish is cooked through. Remove the fish from the milk and set aside to cool slightly. Reserve the milk.
3. In the same pot, melt the butter over medium heat. Add the chopped onion and cook for 5-7 minutes, or until softened.
4. Add the diced potatoes and the reserved milk to the pot. Bring to a boil, then reduce the heat to low and simmer for 20-25 minutes, or until the potatoes are tender.
5. Flake the cooked haddock fillets into bite-sized pieces, discarding any skin and bones.
6. Using an immersion blender or regular blender, blend the potato and milk mixture until smooth. Return the pot to the heat and stir in the flaked haddock, heavy cream, salt, and pepper.
7. Heat the soup until hot, but do not let it boil. Serve hot, garnished with chopped fresh parsley.

Pheasant Pie Recipe

Serves: 6
Prep time: 30 minutes
Cook time: 2 hours

Ingredients:

- 1 pheasant (approx. 700g), deboned and diced
- 1 onion, diced
- 2 garlic cloves, minced
- 2 medium-sized carrots, peeled and diced
- 2 celery stalks, diced
- 2 tbsp olive oil
- 2 tbsp plain flour
- 500ml chicken or vegetable stock
- 150ml red wine
- 2 sprigs of thyme
- 1 bay leaf
- Salt and pepper, to taste
- 500g puff pastry
- 1 egg, beaten

Instructions:

1. Preheat your Instant Vortex Plus Versa Zone on the Bake setting to 200°C.
2. Heat the olive oil in a large saucepan over medium heat.
3. Add the onion, garlic, carrots, and celery, and cook for 5 minutes, or until softened.
4. Add the diced pheasant and cook for another 5 minutes, or until browned.
5. Sprinkle the flour over the mixture and stir well to combine.
6. Gradually add the chicken or vegetable stock and red wine, stirring constantly to avoid lumps.
7. Add the thyme and bay leaf, and season with salt and pepper.
8. Simmer the mixture for 15-20 minutes, or until the sauce has thickened and the vegetables and pheasant are tender.
9. Remove the thyme sprigs and bay leaf. Roll out the puff pastry on a lightly floured surface and cut into a shape that will fit over the top of your pie dish.
10. Transfer the pheasant mixture to a pie dish and cover with the puff pastry, trimming any excess pastry from the edges.
11. Brush the pastry with the beaten egg. Place the pie dish in the Instant Vortex Plus Versa Zone and bake for 30-40 minutes, or until the pastry is golden brown and crispy.
12. Serve

Potted Shrimp Recipe

Serves: 4
Prep time: 10 minutes
Cook time: 20 minutes

Ingredients:

- 200 g unsalted butter
- 2 bay leaves
- 1/2 teaspoon ground mace
- 1/2 teaspoon ground nutmeg
- 1/2 teaspoon ground black pepper
- 1/2 teaspoon cayenne pepper
- 400 g cooked peeled shrimp
- Salt to taste
- Toasted bread or crackers, to serve

Instructions

1. Preheat the Instant Vortex Plus Versa Zone to 100°C.
2. In a small saucepan, melt the butter over low heat. Add the bay leaves, mace, nutmeg, black pepper, and cayenne pepper, and cook for 1-2 minutes, or until fragrant.
3. Remove the bay leaves from the butter and discard.
4. Arrange the cooked peeled shrimp in a small oven-safe dish. Pour the melted butter over the shrimp, making sure they are completely covered.
5. Place the dish in the Instant Vortex Plus Versa Zone and cook for 20 minutes, or until the butter is melted and bubbly.
6. Remove the dish from the Instant Vortex Plus Versa Zone and let it cool to room temperature. Season with salt to taste.
7. Transfer the potted shrimp to a small jar or ramekin and chill in the refrigerator for at least 1 hour, or until set.
8. Serve the potted shrimp cold, with toasted bread or crackers on the side

CHAPTER 3: DINNER

Cornish Pasty

Prep time: 10 minutes + chilling time
Cook time: 30 minutes
Serves 6

Ingredients
- 150g chilled and diced butter
- 150g lard
- 600g plain flour, plus extra
- 1 large egg, beaten

Filling:
- 500g leftover beef, chopped
- 1 shallot, chopped
- 1 medium carrot, shredded
- 300g potatoes, peeled and thinly sliced
- 200g swede, chopped
- Sea salt and ground black pepper, to taste

Instructions
1. Using your fingertips, rub the butter and lard into the flour until the mixture resembles fine breadcrumbs.
2. Now, blend in 8 tbsp cold water to make a firm dough. Cut equally into 6 pieces and chill them for about 30 minutes.
3. In a bowl, thoroughly combine all the filling Ingredients; salt and pepper to taste.
4. On a lightly floured surface, roll out each piece of dough into rounds the size of a tea plate.
5. Divide the filling between pastry circles. Brush the pastry with the beaten egg. Fold the circle in half over the filling and seal the edges. Brush them with the remaining beaten egg.
6. Select "Bake" and set the time for 10 minutes and the temperature to 200 degrees C. Then, lower the temperature to 180 degrees and cook for 20 minutes more until golden. Enjoy!

Sausage Ragu

Prep time: 10 minutes
Cook time: 20 minutes
Serves 5

Ingredients
- 300g pasta of choice
- 1 tbsp olive oil
- 1 medium onion, finely chopped
- 2 garlic cloves, crushed
- 1/2 tsp red pepper flakes
- 1 tbsp dried sage
- 400g canned chopped tomatoes
- 5 cooked pork sausages *or use sausage meat, cooked*
- 100g parmesan, grated

Instructions
1. Cook the pasta according to the pack Instructions.
2. Meanwhile, heat the olive oil in a medium frying pan over medium-high heat. Now, sauté the onion for about 5 minutes, until tender and translucent.
3. Stir in the garlic and continue to cook for a further 30 seconds, until fragrant.
4. Drain the pasta and spoon it into a lightly greased casserole dish. Stir in the sauteed mixture, spices, and chopped tomatoes. Squeeze the sausagemeat from the skins and fold them into the pasta mixture.
5. Select "Bake" and set the time for 15 minutes and the temperature to 180 degrees C.
6. When the display shows "Turn Food", top your casserole with parmesan cheese and rotate the dish; insert the cooking basket

again to continue cooking.
7. Bon appétit!

Garlic Roast Potatoes

Prep time: 5 minutes
Cook time: 15 minutes
Serves 4

Ingredients
- 1kg potatoes, peeled and cut into wedges
- 1 tbsp olive oil
- 1 tbsp freshly squeezed lemon juice
- 2 tbsp garlic, minced
- 2 tsp corn flour
- 1 tsp cayenne pepper
- 1 tsp dried marjoram
- 1 tsp dried oregano
- Sea salt flakes and ground black pepper, to taste

Instructions
1. Add the potatoes along with the other Ingredients to a mixing bowl. Toss until the potatoes are well coated.
2. Then, lower the potatoes into the Air Fryer cooking basket. Select "Air Fry" and set the time for 15 minutes and the temperature to 200 degrees C.
3. When the display shows "Turn Food", shake the basket. Insert the basket again to continue cooking.
4. Bon appétit!

Smoked Mackerel Fishcakes

Prep time: 10 minutes
Cook time: 20 minutes
Serves 5

Ingredients
- 400g small cauliflower florets
- 2 tsp olive oil
- 400g mackerel fillets, skinned and flaked
- 4 spring onions, chopped
- 1 garlic clove, minced
- 1 tbsp horseradish sauce
- 2 tbsp plain flour
- 1 small egg, beaten
- 100g dried breadcrumbs

Instructions
1. Toss cauliflower florets with 1 tsp of olive oil.
2. Then, lower the cauliflower florets into the Air Fryer cooking basket. Select "Air Fry" and set the time for 10 minutes and the temperature to 180 degrees C.
3. When the display shows "Turn Food", shake the basket. Insert the basket again to continue cooking.
4. Mash the cauliflower in a mixing bowl; then, add the other Ingredients and stir to combine well. Next, shape the mixture into 9 to 10 even-sized patties.
5. Lower the fish cakes into the Air Fryer cooking basket. Select "Air Fry" and set the time for 10 minutes and the temperature to 200 degrees C. There is no need to flip the cakes.
6. Serve warm with your favourite sauce for dipping and enjoy!

Sunday Roast

Prep time: 10 minutes + marinating time
Cook time: 40 minutes
Serves 6

Ingredients
- Roast beef:
- 3 pounds beef rump roast
- 4 tbsp sherry wine
- 1 tbsp olive oil
- Sea salt and ground black pepper, to taste

- 1 tsp paprika
- 1 tsp dried parsley flakes
- 1 tsp garlic granules
- 1 tbsp fresh rosemary (optional)

Gravy:
- 2 tbsp butter
- 1 medium onion, sliced
- 3 tablespoons plain flour
- 3 cups beef bone broth

Instructions

1. Pat the beef dry with tea towels. Mix the remaining Ingredients for the roast beef; rub the mixture all over the beef rump roast. Let it marinate in your fridge for about 1 hour.
2. Add beef roast to the Air Fryer cooking basket.
3. Select "Air Fry" and set the time for 40 minutes and the temperature to 190 degrees C.
4. When the display shows "Turn Food", turn the roast over to ensure even cooking. Insert the basket again to continue cooking. When the beef has reached 70 degrees C, it's done.
5. In the meantime, melt the butter in a saucepan over moderately high heat. Now, saute the onions for about 3 minutes, until tender and translucent.
6. Stir in the flour and whisk until it starts to turn a golden colour. Whisk in the beef bone broth; let it simmer until thickened; season with salt and pepper to taste.
7. Carve the roast beef against the grain and serve with warm gravy.
8. Bon appétit!

Egg & Chips

Prep time: 10 minutes
Cook time: 16 minutes
Serves 4

Ingredients

- 1.5kg baking potatoes, cut into wedges
- 2 tsp olive oil
- 1 tsp cayenne pepper
- 1 tsp dried parsley flakes
- Sea salt and ground black pepper, to taste
- 8 eggs

Instructions

1. Toss your potatoes with 1 tsp of olive oil and spices. Tip your potatoes into a roasting tin.
2. Select "Roast" and set the time for 16 minutes and the temperature to 200 degrees C.
3. When the display shows "Turn Food", shake the basket, create 8 spaces in the tin; crack an egg into each one. Drizzle over the remaining 1 teaspoon of oil.
4. Insert the basket again to continue cooking. Serve warm and enjoy!

Salmon in Puff Pastry

Prep time: 10 minutes
Cook time: 25 minutes
Serves 4

Ingredients

- 250g pack puff pastry
- 1 tbsp butter
- 2 cloves garlic, chopped
- 1 small onion, chopped
- 1 tbsp Italian spice mix (optional)
- Sea salt and ground black pepper, to taste
- 100g parmesan cheese
- 400g salmon fillet
- 200g chestnut mushrooms, chopped
- 1 medium egg, beaten

Instructions

1. On a working surface, smooth out the sheet of puff pastry and brush it with butter.
2. Pat fry the salmon fillets with tea towels and sprinkle them with spices. Place the salmon in the middle of the pastry.

3. Place the other Ingredients on top of the salmon, smoothing it out with a spoon.
4. Fold the edges of the puff pastry over the filling; bring the edges together and lower it on the baking tray.
5. Score the top of the pastry with a knife, creating a crosshatch pattern. Brush the top with the beaten egg.
6. Select "Bake" and set the time for 25 minutes and the temperature to 200 degrees C. Enjoy!

Toad in the Hole

Prep time: 10 minutes
Cook time: 40 minutes
Serves 5

Ingredients
- 10 chipolatas
- 150g plain flour
- 1/2 tsp salt
- 2 large eggs
- 180ml milk

Instructions
1. Arrange chipolatas in the roasting tin. Select "Air Fry" and set the time for 15 minutes and the temperature to 180 degrees C.
2. In the meantime, make the batter: Tip the flour into a bowl with salt; then, create a well in the middle and crack the eggs into it.
3. Mix the Ingredients, using your electric whisk; gradually add the milk and mix to combine well; reserve.
4. Pour the batter over your chipolatas and place the roasting tin in your Air Fryer again.
5. Now, select "Bake" and set the time for 25 minutes and the temperature to 200 degrees C. Bake until golden and serve warm. Enjoy!

Cauliflower Cheese

Prep time: 10 minutes
Cook time: 25 minutes
Serves 5

Ingredients
- 1 large cauliflower head, broken into florets
- 400ml full-fat milk
- 4 tbsp plain flour
- 40g butter, melted
- 1 tbsp parsley, chopped
- Ground black pepper, to taste
- A pinch of grated nutmeg
- 120g cheddar cheese, grated
- 2 tbsp breadcrumbs

Instructions
1. Bring a large saucepan of water to a rapid boil. Parboil cauliflower florets for about 5 minutes.
2. Drain the cauliflower florets and tip them into a gratin dish.
3. Heat the milk, flour, butter and spices in a saucepan over low flame. Turn off the heat and stir in the cheese.
4. Then, pour the topping mixture over the cauliflower. Scatter over breadcrumbs and transfer to the Air Fryer.
5. Select "Bake" and set the time for 20 minutes and the temperature to 200 degrees C.
6. When the display shows "Turn Food", rotate the gratin dish to ensure even baking.
7. Insert the basket again to continue cooking. Bake until golden and serve warm.
8. Bon appétit!

Steak and Ale Pie

Prep time: 10 minutes
Cook time: 70 minutes
Serves 6

Ingredients

- 1kg braising steak, diced
- Sea salt and ground black pepper, to taste
- 2 tsp olive oil
- 2 shallots, roughly chopped
- 2 tbsp corn flour
- 2 tbsp sweet chilli sauce
- 200ml sweet brown ale
- 2 thyme sprigs
- 2 bay leaves
- 375g sheet of ready-rolled puff pastry
- 1 small egg, beaten

Instructions

1. Toss braising steak with salt, black pepper, and olive oil.
2. Place the steak in an ovenproof baking dish. Add the shallots, corn flour, sweet chilli, brown ale, thyme, and bay leaves; transfer it to the Air Fryer.
3. Select "Roast" and set the time for 50 minutes and the temperature to 195 degrees C. When the display shows "Turn Food", rotate the dish to ensure even cooking. Discard the thyme and bay leaves.
4. Unroll the puff pastry and drape it over the dish; trim and press the edges against the side of the dish. Brush the top of your pie with the beaten egg.
5. Select "Bake" and set the time for 20 minutes and the temperature to 200 degrees C. When the display shows "Turn Food", rotate the dish to ensure even cooking.
6. Leave the pie to rest for about 10 minutes before serving. Enjoy!

Mini Chicken and Mushroom Pies

Prep time: 10 minutes + chilling time
Cook time: 50 minutes
Serves 6

Ingredients

- Shortcrust pastry:
- 400g all plain flour
- 200g cold butter, cut into chunks
- 1/2 tsp sea salt
- 120ml water, chilled

Filling:
- 1 tbsp olive oil
- 300g brown mushrooms, sliced
- 300g chicken breast, cut into small chunks
- 1 large onion, chopped
- 400ml chicken bone broth (or vegetable broth)
- 100ml double cream
- 1 medium egg

Instructions

1. To make the shortcrust pastry: thoroughly combine all Ingredients until everything is well incorporated.
2. Knead with your hands until the dough is compact and elastic. Shape the dough into a rectangular, and let it chill for about 1 hour in your fridge.
3. Meanwhile, heat olive oil in a large frying pan. Once hot, saute the onion for about 3 minutes, until translucent.
4. Then, cook the chicken chunks for about 5 minutes, until just browned. Now, add the mushrooms and broth; continue to simmer, partially covered, until the chicken is cooked through and the sauce has thickened slightly.
5. Add the cream, stir for about 3 minutes and remove from the heat.
6. On a lightly floured surface, roll out the chilled pastry; cut out 12 circles. Now line 6

non-stick tart tins with 6 circles. Divide the filling between your tins.
7. Cover them with the remaining pastry circles, pressing the edges gently to prevent any leakage.
8. Beat the egg with 1 tablespoon of water to make the egg wash. Brush the pies with the egg wash and lower them into the Air Fryer cooking basket.
9. Select "Bake" and set the time for 40 minutes and the temperature to 190 degrees C. When the display shows "Turn Food", rotate tart tins to ensure even baking.
10. Bon appétit!

Old-Fashioned Liver and Onions

Prep time: 10 minutes
Cook time: 12 minutes
Serves 5

Ingredients
- 2 tbsp plain flour
- 1 tsp garlic granules
- 1 tsp cayenne pepper
- Sea salt and ground black pepper, to taste
- 500g chicken livers
- 1 tbsp olive oil
- 5 rashers smoked streaky bacon
- 1 medium onion, sliced

Instructions
1. Slide the tray divider into the cooking tray. Put the cooking basket into the Air Fryer and then, press the Control Dial two times quickly to activate Dual Zone cooking.
2. Mix the flour with spices and set it aside. Dust the liver with the flour mixture. Brush it with olive oil and lower it into Drawer 1 of your Air Fryer. Select "Air Fry" on this drawer and set the temperature to 195 degrees C and the time to 12 minutes.
3. Place the bacon and onion in Drawer 2. Select "Air Fry", and set the temperature to 200 degrees C and the time to 7 minutes. Select "SyncFinish" to ensure both drawers finish at the same time.
4. When the display shows "Turn Food", remove the cooking basket and carefully flip your food. Insert the basket again to continue cooking.
5. Bon appétit!

Scampi with Tartare Sauce

Prep time: 10 minutes
Cook time: 7 minutes
Serves 6

Ingredients
- 100g plain flour
- 50g cornflour
- Sea salt and ground black pepper, to taste
- 100ml stout
- 50ml plain milk
- 18 Dublin Bay prawn tails
- 100g fresh breadcrumbs
- 1 tbsp olive oil

Tartare sauce:
- 1 gherkin, finely chopped
- 1 tbsp fresh parsley, chopped
- 1 tbsp fresh tarragon, chopped
- 6 tbsp mayonnaise
- 1 tsp lemon juice

Instructions
1. Mix both types of flour in a shallow bowl along with salt and pepper. Add stout and milk, and whisk to a smooth batter.
2. Dip prawn tails into the batter. Roll them over the fresh breadcrumbs. Now, brush prawn tails with the oil and arrange them in the Air Fryer cooking basket
3. Select "Air Fry" and set the time for 7

minutes and the temperature to 200 degrees C. When the display shows "Turn Food", shake the basket. Insert the basket again to continue cooking.
4. Meanwhile, mix all Ingredients for the tartare sauce.
5. Serve your scampi with the tartare sauce on the side and enjoy!

Butter-Basted Roast Chicken

Prep time: 10 minutes
Cook time: 1 hour
Serves 6

Ingredients
- 50g butter, softened
- 1 bunch of lemon thyme, leaves picked
- Sea salt and ground black pepper, to taste
- 2 garlic cloves, smashed
- 2 garlic cloves, slivered
- 1 lemon, juiced
- 2kg chicken
- 1 large leek, sliced
- 2 large carrots, sliced

Instructions
1. Mix the butter with lemon thyme, salt, pepper, smashed garlic, and lemon juice; set it aside.
2. Rub the butter mixture all over the outside of the chicken, then stuff the cavity with the slivered garlic.
3. Slide the tray divider into the cooking tray. Put the cooking basket into the Air Fryer and then, press the Control Dial two times quickly to activate Dual Zone cooking.
4. Lower the chicken into Drawer 1 of your Air Fryer. Select "Roast" on this drawer and set the temperature to 180 degrees C and the time to 1 hour.
5. Place the carrots and leek in Drawer 2. Select "Air Fry", and set the temperature to 190 degrees C and the time to 15 minutes. Select "SyncFinish" to ensure both drawers finish at the same time.
6. Let the chicken rest for about 10 minutes before carving. Serve it with the vegetables on the side and enjoy!

Irish Soda Bread

Prep time: 10 minutes
Cook time: 35 minutes
Serves 6

Ingredients
- 250g plain wholemeal flour
- 300g plain flour
- 90g porridge oats
- 1 tsp bicarbonate of soda
- 1 tsp salt
- 20g cold butter, cut into pieces
- 550ml buttermilk

Instructions
1. In a mixing bowl, thoroughly combine dry Ingredients; now, rub in the butter.
2. Add the buttermilk to the bowl and mix it using a table knife. After that, bring the dough together using your fingertips (do it gently).
3. Shape your dough into a loaf and lower it onto a baking pan; score a deep cross on the top.
4. Select "Bake" and set the time for 35 minutes and the temperature to 200 degrees C. When the display shows "Turn Food", rotate the baking pan. Insert the basket again to continue baking.
5. Transfer your bread to a wire rack and cover it with a tea towel. Leave it to rest for 10 minutes before slicing and serving.
6. Bon appétit!

Authentic Glamorgan Sausages

Prep time: 10 minutes + chilling time
Cook time: 15 minutes
Serves 6

Ingredients
- 500g fresh breadcrumbs
- 50g butter
- 2 medium leeks, sliced
- 4 medium eggs, separated
- 400g cheddar cheese, finely grated
- 1 tbsp English mustard
- 50g plain flour
- 1 tbsp olive oil

Instructions
1. In a mixing bowl, thoroughly combine 1/2 of the breadcrumbs, butter, leeks, egg yolks, cheese, and mustard.
2. Mould the mixture into 10 to 12 sausages; chill them for about 1 hour in your fridge.
3. Meanwhile, whisk the egg whites in a shallow bowl, and add the flour to another bowl.
4. Dust the sausages in the flour, then dunk in the egg white. Afterwards, roll them over the breadcrumbs. Chill the sausages overnight in your fridge.
5. On an actual day, add the sausages to the Air Fryer cooking basket and brash them with olive oil.
6. Select "Air Fry" and set the time for 15 minutes and the temperature to 190 degrees C.
7. When the display shows "Turn Food", turn the sausages over to ensure even cooking. Insert the basket again to continue cooking. Enjoy!

Mom's Baked Risotto

Prep time: 10 minutes
Cook time: 20 minutes
Serves 6

Ingredients
- 1 tbsp olive oil
- 200g smoked bacon, chopped
- 1 shallot, chopped
- 350g risotto rice
- 50ml sherry wine
- 600ml hot chicken broth
- 1 large tomato, chopped
- 60g parmesan cheese, preferably freshly grated

Instructions
1. Mix olive oil, bacon, and shallot in an ovenproof pan. Tip in the rice; stir to combine well. Pour over the wine and broth.
2. Fold in the tomatoes and give them a good stir. Cover with foil and transfer to the Air Fryer cooking basket.
3. Select "Bake" and set the time for 20 minutes and the temperature to 200 degrees C.
4. When the display shows "Turn Food", stir your risotto to ensure even cooking. Top your risotto with cheese and insert the basket again to continue cooking.
5. Bon appétit!

Country-Style Sausage Casserole

Prep time: 10 minutes
Cook time: 25 minutes
Serves 6

Ingredients
- 1 tbsp olive
- 1 onion, finely chopped

- 2 medium carrots, finely chopped
- 1 bell pepper, chopped
- 700g cooking sausages (Chorizo-style or Italian sausages)
- 2 garlic cloves, chopped
- 1 tsp dried parsley flakes
- 1 tsp paprika
- 1/2 tsp ground cumin
- 100ml white wine
- 100ml water
- 1 (400g) can of crushed tomatoes
- 1 chicken stock cube
- 1 (400g) can of red beans, drained and rinsed

Instructions

1. Heat the olive oil in a large heavy-based frying pan over a medium-high flame. Sauté the onion for 5 minutes, until tender and translucent.
2. Add carrots and bell pepper, and continue sauteing for a further 5 minutes, until they've softened.
3. Add the sauteed mixture to a lightly greased casserole dish. Add the remaining Ingredients and gently stir to combine.
4. Select "Bake" and set the time for 15 minutes and the temperature to 180 degrees C.
5. When the display shows "Turn Food", rotate the dish; insert the basket again to continue cooking.
6. Serve warm and enjoy!

Crispy Roast Pork Belly

Prep time: 10 minutes
Cook time: 40 minutes
Serves 8

Ingredients
- 2kg pork belly, ribs intact, skin scored
- 1 tsp cumin seeds
- 1 tsp mustard seeds
- 1 tsp coriander seeds
- 1 tsp chilli flakes
- 1 tbsp sea salt flakes
- 1 small lemon, juiced
- 50ml dry vermouth
- Roasted Baby Carrots:
- 1kg baby carrots, trimmed
- Sea salt and cayenne pepper, to taste
- 1 tsp dried dill weed
- 1 tsp olive oil

Instructions

1. Pat pork belly dry with tea towels. Rub spices into the skin, ensuring it goes into the scores. Drizzle the pork belly with lemon juice and vermouth.
2. Lower the pork belly skin side up on a kitchen foil; wrap the sides of the foil up to enclose the pork belly. Be sure the corners are folded tightly together.
3. Lower the pork belly into Drawer 1 of your Air Fryer. Select "Air Fry" on this drawer and set the temperature to 160 degrees C and the time to 30 minutes.
4. Toss the carrots with salt, cayenne pepper, dill, and olive oil. Place the carrots in Drawer 2. Select "SyncCook" to automatically mirror the settings in Drawer 2.
5. When the display shows "Turn Food", remove the cooking basket and carefully flip your food. Insert the basket again to continue cooking.
6. When the time is up, remove the baby carrots from the cooking basket and reserve them. Now, turn the temperature up to 195 degrees C, and air fry pork belly for a further 10 minutes.
7. At the halfway point, check to see whether the crackling is done to your liking. Leave the meat to rest for 5 minutes to allow the juices to reabsorb. Serve warm pork belly with roasted baby carrots on the side and enjoy!

Fish Mornay

Prep time: 10 minutes
Cook time: 25 minutes
Serves 4

Ingredients

- 1 tsp olive oil
- 600g white fish fillets (tilapia, cod or Sea bass)
- 600ml milk
- 60g butter
- 60g plain flour
- Sea salt and freshly ground black pepper, to taste
- 1/2 tsp red pepper flakes
- 1 tsp dried oregano
- 1/2 tsp dried basil
- 1 tsp dried parsley flakes
- 1/2 tsp garlic granules
- 160g cheddar

Instructions

1. Brush the interior of a casserole dish with olive oil. Lower the fish into the dishes.
2. Then, heat the flour, butter and milk in a medium saucepan over moderately high heat, whisking constantly to break up the potential lumps.
3. Cook until the sauce has thickened; heat off. Add spices and grate the cheese to the sauce; whisk until the cheese has melted.
4. Spoon the sauce evenly over the fish fillets and transfer the casserole dish to the Air Fryer cooking basket.
5. Select "Bake" and set the time for 18 minutes and the temperature to 180 degrees C.
6. When the display shows "Turn Food", rotate the dish; insert the cooking basket again to continue cooking.
7. Serve immediately and enjoy!

Tomato Pasta Traybake

Prep time: 10 minutes
Cook time: 20 minutes
Serves 4

Ingredients

- 200g rigatoni pasta
- 1 tbsp olive oil
- 1 onion, chopped
- 1 garlic clove, crushed
- 2 bell peppers, chopped
- 2 (400g) cans chopped tomatoes
- 100g cheddar, grated
- A hunk of baguette, torn into pieces

Instructions

1. Cook the pasta according to the pack Instructions.
2. Meanwhile, heat the olive oil in a medium frying pan over medium-high heat. Now, sauté the onion for about 5 minutes, until tender and translucent.
3. Stir in the garlic and peppers; cook for a further 30 seconds, until fragrant.
4. Drain the pasta and spoon it into a lightly greased casserole dish. Stir in the sauteed mixture and chopped tomatoes.
5. Top your casserole with cheese and baguette pieces.
6. Select "Bake" and set the time for 15 minutes and the temperature to 180 degrees C.
7. When the display shows "Turn Food", rotate the dish; insert the cooking basket again to continue cooking.
8. Bon appétit!

Vegan Jacket Potatoes

Prep time: 10 minutes
Cook time: 35 minutes
Serves 5

Ingredients

- 5 sweet potatoes
- 1 tbsp olive oil
- 250g canned or cooked chickpeas, drained and rinsed
- 1 medium bell pepper, chopped
- 1 chilli pepper, chopped
- 1 large shallot, diced
- 2 garlic cloves, crushed
- 1 tsp garam masala
- 1 tsp ground coriander
- 1 large tomato, chopped

Instruction

1. Prick the sweet potatoes all over with a fork.
2. Select "Roast" and set the time for 25 minutes and the temperature to 170 degrees C.
3. In a mixing bowl, thoroughly combine the other Ingredients.
4. Put the roasted potatoes on a baking tray and cut them open lengthways. Spoon over the chickpea mixture.
5. Select "Roast" and set the time for 10 minutes and the temperature to 180 degrees C. There is no need to flip the food.
6. Bon appétit!

The Best Haslet Ever

Prep time: 10 minutes
Cook time: 35 minutes
Serves 5

Ingredients

- 4 slices day-old white bread, in cubes
- 100ml milk
- 1kg pork mince
- 1 medium shallot, chopped
- 1 tsp fresh sage, chopped
- Sea salt and ground black pepper, to taste
- 1 tsp cayenne pepper
- 1 smoked paprika

Instructions

1. Lightly grease a loaf tin. Soak cubed bread in milk and then, squeeze out excess moisture. Add the other Ingredients and stir to combine well.
2. Place the mixture in the prepared tin, pressing down evenly. Cover with a piece of foil and lower your haslet into the Air Fryer cooking basket.
3. Select "Bake" and set the time for 35 minutes and the temperature to 200 degrees C.
4. When the display shows "Turn Food", remove the foil; insert the cooking basket again to continue cooking.
5. Bon appétit!

Somerset Chicken

Prep time: 10 minutes
Cook time: 25 minutes
Serves 4

Ingredients

- 1kg chicken breasts, skin on, boneless
- Sea salt and freshly ground black pepper, to taste
- 1 tsp cayenne pepper
- 4 large potatoes, peeled and quartered
- 1 tsp olive oil
- 20g butter, room temperature
- 2 onions, chopped
- 1 tbsp wholegrain mustard
- 2 dessert apples, peeled, sliced into batons
- 100g button mushrooms, sliced
- 100ml cider

- 100ml double cream *use yoghurt as crème fraîche*
- 100g cheddar cheese, grated

Instructions

1. Slide the tray divider into the cooking tray. Put the cooking basket into the Air Fryer and then, press the Control Dial two times quickly to activate Dual Zone cooking.
2. Season the chicken with salt, black pepper, and cayenne pepper and place it in a roasting tin; lower the chicken into Drawer 1 of your Air Fryer.
3. Select "Roast" on this drawer and set the temperature to 200 degrees C and the time to 25 minutes.
4. Toss the potatoes with salt, pepper, and olive oil. Place the potatoes in Drawer 2. Select "SyncCook" to automatically mirror the settings in Drawer 2.
5. When the display shows "Turn Food", remove the cooking basket and carefully flip your food. Top the chicken breasts with butter, onions, mustard, apples, mushrooms, cider, cream, and cheese.
6. Insert the basket again to continue cooking.
7. Bon appétit!

Chicken Parmo

Serves 4
Prep time: 10 minutes
Cook time: 27 minutes

Ingredients

- 400g chicken fillets
- Sea salt and ground black pepper, to taste
- 1 tsp paprika
- 1 tsp dried parsley flakes
- 50g plain flour
- 2 large eggs, beaten
- 1 tsp olive oil
- 200g dried breadcrumbs
- Béchamel Sauce Topping:
- 50g butter
- 50g plain flour
- 350ml milk
- A pinch of grated nutmeg
- 100g Gruyère cheese, grated

Instructions

1. Pat the chicken fillets dry with tea towels. Season the chicken with salt, black pepper, and parsley.
2. Place the flour, eggs and breadcrumbs in 3 separate shallow bowls. Now, dip the chicken fillets in flour, egg and breadcrumbs; press to coat.
3. Lower the chicken into the cooking basket and drizzle with olive oil.
4. Select "Bake" and set the time for 20 minutes and the temperature to 200 degrees C. When the display shows "Turn Food", remove the cooking basket and carefully flip the fillets to ensure even cooking. Arrange the chicken in a lightly greased baking tray.
5. Meanwhile, make the béchamel sauce topping. Melt the butter in a saucepan, then, cook the flour until smooth. Gradually whisk in the milk, and let it simmer for approximately 5 minutes until the sauce has thicked; add nutmeg and cheese. Salt to taste and reserve.
6. Spoon the béchamel sauce topping over each chicken breast and lower the baking tray into the cooking basket. Select "Bake" and set the time for 7 minutes and the temperature to 200 degrees C. Enjoy!

Chicken Korma

Pressure Cooked

Serves: 4-6
Prep time: 15 minutes
Cook time: 30 minutes

Ingredients:
- 1200g boneless, skinless chicken breasts, cut into bite-sized pieces
- 2 tbsp ghee or butter
- 2 onions, chopped
- 4 garlic cloves, minced
- 1 tbsp grated fresh ginger
- 2 tsp ground coriander
- 2 tsp ground cumin
- 2 tsp garam masala
- 1 tsp turmeric powder
- 1/2 tsp cayenne pepper
- 400 ml coconut milk
- 400 ml canned tomato sauce
- 200 ml plain Greek yogurt
- 2 tsp salt, or to taste
- Fresh cilantro, chopped for garnish

Instructions
1. Set the instant vortex plus versa zone to 180°c and add the ghee or butter. Once melted, add the onions and cook until softened.
2. Add the garlic and ginger and cook for 1-2 minutes, or until fragrant.
3. Add the ground coriander, cumin, garam masala, turmeric, and cayenne pepper and stir to combine.
4. Add the chicken to the pot and stir to coat it with the spices.
5. Add the coconut milk, canned tomato sauce, and salt to the pot and stir until well combined.
6. Close the Instant Pot lid, turn the valve to sealing, and press the Manual button. Set the cooking time for 15 minutes on high pressure.
7. Once the cooking time is complete, allow the pressure to release naturally for 10 minutes before carefully turning the valve to venting to release any remaining pressure.
8. Remove the lid and stir in the Greek yogurt

Chicken Fettuccine Alfredo

Pressure Cooker

Serves: 4
Prep time: 10 minutes
Cook time: 20 minutes

Ingredients:
- 400g fettuccine pasta
- 450g boneless, skinless chicken breasts, cut into small pieces
- 4 tbsp unsalted butter
- heavy cream (480ml)
- freshly grated parmesan cheese (100g)
- Salt and pepper to taste
- Chopped fresh parsley for garnish

Instructions
1. Cook the fettuccine pasta according to the package Instructions. Drain and set aside.
2. In a large pan, heat the butter over medium heat until melted in the Instant Vortex Plus Versa Zone at 180°c
3. Add the chicken pieces to the pan and cook until browned on all sides, about 5-6 minutes.
4. Pour the heavy cream into the pan and stir to combine with the chicken and butter. Bring to a simmer and cook for 5-6 minutes, stirring occasionally.
5. Add the parmesan cheese to the pan and stir until melted and combined with the sauce.
6. Season with salt and pepper to taste.
7. Add the cooked fettuccine to the pan and toss to coat with the sauce.
8. Serve hot, garnished with chopped fresh parsley.

Pressure cooked

Instant Pot Chicken Adobo

Serves: 4
Prep time: 10 minutes
Cook time: 20 minutes

Ingredients:

- 1200g bone-in chicken thighs
- soy sauce (120ml)
- Vinegar (120ml)
- Brown sugar (50g)
- Water (60ml)
- 6 cloves garlic, minced
- 1 tsp black pepper
- 1 bay leaf

Instructions

1. Combine the soy sauce, vinegar, brown sugar, water, minced garlic, black pepper, and bay leaf in the Instant Pot and stir to combine.
2. Add the chicken thighs to the Instant Pot and turn to coat with the sauce.
3. Close the Instant Pot lid and turn the valve to the sealing position.
4. Heat the Instant Vortex Plus Versa Zone at about 180°c a and Cook on high pressure for 20 minutes.
5. When the cooking time is complete, allow the pressure to release naturally for 10 minutes before using the quick release to release any remaining pressure.
6. Remove the chicken from the Instant Pot and set aside.
7. Turn on the Instant Pot to about 120°c and cook the sauce until it thickens to your desired consistency.
8. Serve the chicken with the sauce spooned over the top.

Pressure cooks

Instant Pot Pork Carnitas

Serves: 8-10
Prep time: 10 minutes
Cook Time: 1 hour, 20 minutes

long cooking time

Ingredients:

- 1500g pork shoulder, cut into 2-inch cubes
- 1 tablespoon olive oil
- 1 teaspoon salt
- 1 teaspoon pepper
- 1 teaspoon cumin
- 1 teaspoon chili powder
- 1 teaspoon garlic powder
- 1 onion, diced
- 4 cloves garlic, minced
- orange juice (120 ml)
- lime juice (60 ml)
- chicken broth (60 ml)

Instructions

1. In a small bowl, mix together salt, pepper, cumin, chili powder, and garlic powder. Rub the spice mixture all over the pork cubes.
2. Set Instant Pot to 120°c mode and add olive oil. Once heated, brown the pork cubes on all sides, about 2-3 minutes per side.
3. Add diced onion and minced garlic to the Instant Pot and heat for 2-3 minutes.
4. Add orange juice, lime juice, and chicken broth to the Instant Pot. Use a wooden spoon to scrape any brown bits from the bottom of the pot.
5. Close the Instant Pot lid and set it to manual pressure cook for 1 hour and 15 minutes. After cooking, allow for natural pressure release for 10-15 minutes.
6. Remove the pork cubes from the Instant Pot and shred with two forks. Return the shredded pork to the Instant Pot and toss it in the remaining liquid.
7. Set the Instant Pot to about 120°c mode and

cook the pork for an additional 5-7 minutes, stirring occasionally, until the liquid has reduced and the pork is crispy.

Beef Gyros

Serves: 4
Prep time: 10 minutes
Cook Time: 20 minutes

Ingredients:
- 500 g beef sirloin, sliced thinly
- 1 tablespoon olive oil
- 1 teaspoon salt
- 1 teaspoon pepper
- 1 teaspoon oregano
- 1 teaspoon thyme
- 1 onion, sliced
- 2 cloves garlic, minced
- 4 pita breads
- tzatziki sauce (60 ml)
- diced tomatoes (60 g)
- diced cucumber (60 g)

Instructions

1. In a small bowl, mix together salt, pepper, oregano, and thyme. Rub the spice mixture all over the sliced beef.
2. Set Instant Vortex Plus Versa Zone to air fry mode at 200°C for 10 minutes. Once heated, add olive oil and sliced beef to the cooking basket. Cook for 5-7 minutes or until the beef is browned and crispy.
3. Remove the beef from the cooking basket and set aside.
4. Add sliced onion and minced garlic to the cooking basket and cook for 3-4 minutes, until softened.
5. Warm up the pita breads in the Instant Vortex Plus Versa Zone at 150°C for 2 minutes.
6. To assemble the gyros, spread tzatziki sauce on the pita breads, add the cooked beef, onions, tomatoes, and cucumbers. Roll the pita bread tightly and serve.

Chicken Teriyaki

Serves: 4
Prep time: 10 minutes
Cook time: 20 minutes

Ingredients:
- 4 boneless, skinless chicken breasts (600g)
- 80 ml soy sauce
- 60 ml mirin
- 40 ml sake
- 40 g brown sugar
- 2 cloves garlic, minced
- 1 tbsp ginger, minced
- 1 tbsp cornstarch
- 20 ml water
- Sesame seeds, for garnish

Instructions

1. In a bowl, mix together the soy sauce, mirin, sake, brown sugar, garlic, and ginger.
2. Place the chicken breasts in the marinade and let sit for at least 10 minutes.
3. In a small bowl, whisk together the cornstarch and water until smooth.
4. Preheat the Instant Vortex Plus Versa Zone to 200°C.
5. Remove the chicken from the marinade and place on the cooking tray.
6. Place the cooking tray in the Instant Vortex Plus Versa Zone and cook for 12 minutes.
7. After 12 minutes, remove the cooking tray from the oven and brush the chicken with some of the remaining marinade.
8. Return the cooking tray to the Instant Vortex Plus Versa Zone and cook for an additional 8 minutes or until the chicken is fully cooked.
9. Remove the chicken from the oven and let rest for a few minutes before slicing.

10. Serve the chicken with any remaining marinade drizzled over the top and garnished with sesame seeds. Enjoy

Sloppy Joes

Mainly using microwave

Serves: 4-6
Prep time: 10 minutes
Cook time: 20 minutes

Ingredients:
- 500g ground beef
- 1 small onion, chopped
- 1 small green bell pepper, chopped
- 2 cloves garlic, minced
- (400g) diced tomatoes
- 60 ml ketchup
- 30 ml tomato paste
- 30 ml Worcestershire sauce
- 15 g brown sugar
- 5 ml yellow mustard
- Salt and pepper, to taste
- 4-6 hamburger buns

Instructions
1. Preheat the Instant Vortex Plus Versa Zone to 190°C.
2. In a large skillet over medium heat, brown the ground beef.
3. Once the beef is browned, add the onion, green bell pepper, and garlic to the skillet and cook until the vegetables are softened.
4. Add the diced tomatoes, ketchup, tomato paste, Worcestershire sauce, brown sugar, and yellow mustard to the skillet. Mix well.
5. Reduce the heat to low and let the mixture simmer for 10 minutes, stirring occasionally.
6. While the mixture is simmering, place the hamburger buns in the Instant Vortex Plus Versa Zone and toast for 2-3 minutes, until lightly golden.
7. Once the mixture is done simmering, season with salt and pepper to taste.
8. Remove the hamburger buns from the Instant Vortex Plus Versa Zone and place the bottom halves on plates.
9. Spoon the Sloppy Joe mixture onto the hamburger buns and top with the other half of the bun.
10. Serve hot and enjoy your delicious Sloppy Joes

Corn chowder

Probably use pressure cooker

Serves: 4-6
Prep time: 10 minutes
Cook time: 20 minutes

Ingredients:
- 30 g butter
- 1 small onion, diced
- 1 small red bell pepper, diced
- 2 cloves garlic, minced
- (475 ml) chicken broth
- 500g frozen corn kernels
- 2 medium potatoes, peeled and diced
- 1/4 tsp dried thyme
- 250 ml heavy cream
- Salt and pepper, to taste
- 2 tbsp chopped fresh parsley, for garnish

Instructions
1. Preheat the Instant Vortex Plus Versa Zone to 180°C.
2. Add the butter to the cooking pot and let it melt.
3. Add the diced onion, red bell pepper, and minced garlic to the pot and heat until softened.
4. Add the chicken broth, frozen corn, diced potatoes, and dried thyme to the pot. Mix well.
5. Close the lid of the Instant Vortex Plus Versa Zone and select the Soup function. Set the cooking time for 20 minutes.

6. Once the cooking time is up, carefully release the pressure and remove the lid.
7. Stir in the heavy cream and season with salt and pepper to taste.
8. Select the Saute function again and let the chowder simmer for a few minutes to thicken up.
9. Serve the corn chowder hot, garnished with chopped fresh parsley.

Chicken Parmesan

Serves: 4
Prep time: 15 minutes
Cook time: 20 minutes

Ingredients:

- 4 boneless, skinless chicken breasts (about 500g)
- 120 g all-purpose flour
- 2 large eggs
- 60 ml milk
- 200 g seasoned breadcrumbs
- 60 g grated Parmesan cheese
- 750 ml marinara sauce
- 200 g shredded mozzarella cheese
- Salt and pepper, to taste
- Fresh basil leaves, for garnish

Instructions

1. Preheat the Instant Vortex Plus Versa Zone to 190°C.
2. Set up a breading station by placing the flour in a shallow dish, whisking the eggs and milk together in a second shallow dish, and mixing the breadcrumbs and grated Parmesan cheese in a third shallow dish.
3. Season the chicken breasts with salt and pepper.
4. Dredge each chicken breast in the flour, shaking off any excess.
5. Dip each chicken breast in the egg mixture, then coat in the breadcrumb mixture, pressing the crumbs onto the chicken to ensure even coverage.
6. Place the breaded chicken breasts in the Instant Vortex Plus Versa Zone basket and spray with cooking spray.
7. Cook the chicken for 10 minutes, then flip and cook for another 10 minutes, or until the chicken is cooked through and the breadcrumbs are golden brown.
8. Pour the marinara sauce over the chicken breasts, then sprinkle the shredded mozzarella cheese on top.
9. Place the basket back in the Instant Vortex Plus Versa Zone and cook for an additional 5-7 minutes, or until the cheese is melted and bubbly.
10. Serve the chicken parmesan hot, garnished with fresh basil leaves.

Baked Ziti *(Tubular Pasta)*

mainly using microwave until Stage 10.

Serves: 4-6
Prep time: 20 minutes
Cook time: 25 minutes

Ingredients:

- 500g ziti pasta
- 500g ground beef *minced beef*
- 1 onion, chopped
- 4 garlic cloves, minced
- 800g canned crushed tomatoes
- 240ml water
- 1 tablespoon dried basil
- 1 tablespoon dried oregano
- Salt and pepper, to taste
- 340g shredded mozzarella cheese
- 100g grated Parmesan cheese

Instructions

1. Preheat the Instant Vortex Plus Versa Zone to 180°C

2. Cook the ziti pasta according to the package Instructions until al dente. Drain and set aside.
3. In a large skillet, brown the ground beef over medium-high heat, breaking it up into small pieces as it cooks.
4. Add the chopped onion and minced garlic to the skillet and cook for an additional 2-3 minutes, or until the onion is translucent and the garlic is fragrant.
5. Add the canned crushed tomatoes, water, dried basil, dried oregano, salt, and pepper to the skillet, and stir well to combine.
6. Simmer the sauce for 10-15 minutes, stirring occasionally, until it has thickened slightly.
7. In a large mixing bowl, combine the cooked ziti pasta and the sauce, and mix well to ensure that the pasta is coated evenly.
8. Transfer the pasta and sauce mixture to a 9x13 inch baking dish.
9. Sprinkle the shredded mozzarella cheese and grated Parmesan cheese over the top of the pasta.
10. Bake the ziti in the Instant Vortex Plus Versa Zone for 25 minutes, or until the cheese is melted and bubbly and the pasta is heated through.
11. Remove the ziti from the oven and allow it to cool for a few minutes before serving

Goulash

?? using pressure cooker.

Serves: 4-6
Prep time: 20 minutes
Cook Time: 1 hour 30 minutes

Ingredients:
- 800 g beef chuck roast, cut into 2-inch pieces
- 2 onions, chopped
- 2 red bell peppers, chopped
- 2 tablespoons paprika
- 2 teaspoons caraway seeds
- 2 garlic cloves, minced
- 1 tablespoon tomato paste
- beef broth
- 50ml of water
- 2 tablespoons all-purpose flour
- 2 tablespoons vegetable oil
- Salt and pepper, to taste

Instructions
1. Preheat the Instant Vortex Plus Versa Zone to 150°C.
2. In a large bowl, season the beef with salt and pepper. Add flour and toss to coat.
3. Heat oil in the Instant Vortex Plus Versa Zone using the Saute function. Add the beef and cook until browned on all sides. Remove beef and set aside.
4. Add onions, bell peppers, garlic, paprika, caraway seeds, and tomato paste to the pot. Cook for 5 minutes until vegetables are softened.
5. Add beef broth and water, and return beef to the pot. Stir well to combine.
6. Close the lid of the Instant Vortex Plus Versa Zone and cook for 1 hour.
7. After 1 hour, open the lid and check the consistency of the goulash. If it's too thick, add more water. If it's too thin, leave it to cook for a further 10-15 minutes with the lid off.
8. Serve hot with crusty bread or over cooked potatoes or egg noodles.

Braised Oxtail Recipe

Serves: 4-6
Prep time: 20 minutes
Cook Time: 3 hours

Ingredients:
- 1000g oxtail
- 2 onions, chopped

- 2 carrots, chopped
- 2 celery stalks, chopped
- 4 garlic cloves, minced
- 2 bay leaves
- 2 sprigs of fresh thyme
- 2 tablespoons tomato paste
- 1 tablespoon Worcestershire sauce
- 1 tablespoon all-purpose flour
- 400ml beef broth
- 200ml red wine
- 2 tablespoons vegetable oil
- Salt and pepper, to taste

Instructions

1. Preheat the Instant Vortex Plus Versa Zone to 150°C
2. In a large bowl, season the oxtail with salt and pepper. Add flour and toss to coat.
3. Heat oil in the Instant Vortex Plus Versa Zone using the Saute function. Add the oxtail and cook until browned on all sides. Remove oxtail and set aside.
4. Add onions, carrots, celery, and garlic to the pot. Cook for 5 minutes until vegetables are softened.
5. Add tomato paste, Worcestershire sauce, bay leaves, and thyme to the pot. Stir well to combine.
6. Add beef broth and red wine to the pot, and return the oxtail to the pot. Stir well to combine.
7. Close the lid of the Instant Vortex Plus Versa Zone and cook for 3 hours.
8. After 3 hours, open the lid and check the consistency of the braised oxtail. If it's too thick, add more water. If it's too thin, leave it to cook for a further 10-15 minutes with the lid off.
9. Serve hot with mashed potatoes, rice or crusty bread.

Venison Stew

Serves: 4-6
Prep time: 20 minutes
Cook time: 3 hours

- 1000g venison stew meat, cubed
- 2 tbsp olive oil
- 1 onion, chopped
- 2 carrots, chopped
- 2 celery stalks, chopped
- 2 cloves garlic, minced
- 1 tbsp tomato paste
- 400ml beef or venison broth
- 200ml of red wine
- 1 bay leaf
- 1 sprig fresh thyme
- Salt and pepper to taste

Instructions

1. Preheat the Instant Vortex Plus Versa Zone to 150°C.
2. In a large pot heat the olive oil over medium-high heat.
3. Add the venison cubes and brown on all sides, about 5 minutes.
4. Remove the venison from the pot and set aside.
5. Add the onion, carrots, and celery to the pot and sauté until they start to soften, about 5 minutes.
6. Add the garlic and tomato paste and cook for another minute.
7. Add the beef or venison broth, red wine, bay leaf, thyme, salt, and pepper to the pot and bring to a simmer.
8. Add the browned venison back into the pot, cover with a lid, and transfer to the Instant Vortex Plus Versa Zone.
9. Cook for 3 hours or until the venison is tender. Adjust seasoning to taste and serve hot.

?? how you would cook this in an airfryer

Steak and Stilton Pie

Serves: 4-6
Prep time: 20 minutes
Cook time: 1 hour

Ingredients:

- 500g beef sirloin steak, cubed
- 2 tbsp olive oil
- 1 onion, chopped
- 2 cloves garlic, minced
- 2 tbsp flour
- 400ml beef broth
- 1 tbsp Worcestershire sauce
- 1 tbsp tomato paste
- 1 sprig fresh thyme
- Salt and pepper to taste
- 200g Stilton cheese, crumbled
- 1 sheet puff pastry
- 1 egg, beaten

Instructions

1. Preheat the Instant Vortex Plus Versa Zone to 180°C.
2. In a large pot or Dutch oven, heat the olive oil over medium-high heat.
3. Add the beef cubes and brown on all sides, about 5 minutes. Remove the beef from the pot and set aside.
4. Add the onion and garlic to the pot and sauté until they start to soften, about 5 minutes.
5. Add the flour and cook for another minute.
6. Add the beef broth, Worcestershire sauce, tomato paste, thyme, salt, and pepper to the pot and bring to a simmer.
7. Add the browned beef back into the pot and cook for another 10 minutes.
8. Transfer the beef and sauce into a pie dish and sprinkle the Stilton cheese on top.
9. Roll out the puff pastry and cover the top of the pie dish, trimming any excess pastry.
10. Brush the beaten egg over the top of the pastry.
11. Cut a small hole in the center of the pastry to allow steam to escape.
12. Transfer the pie to the Instant Vortex Plus Versa Zone and cook for 45-60 minutes, or until the pastry is golden brown and the filling is hot and bubbly.
13. Let the pie cool for a few minutes before serving

Stuffed Bell peppers with Quinoa and Grounded Beef

Serves: 4
Prep time: 20 minutes
Cook Time: 35 minutes

Ingredients:

- 4 large bell peppers, tops removed and seeds removed
- 2 tbsp olive oil
- 1 onion, finely chopped
- 2 garlic cloves, minced
- 250g minced beef
- cooked quinoa
- diced tomatoes (400g)
- 1 tsp dried oregano
- 1 tsp dried basil
- Salt and pepper, to taste
- 100g feta cheese, crumbled
- Fresh parsley, chopped for garnish

Instructions

1. Preheat your Instant Vortex Plus Versa Zone to 180°C.
2. In a large pot, cook the bell peppers in boiling salted water for 5 minutes. Drain and set aside.
3. In a large frying pan, heat the olive oil over medium heat. Add the chopped onion and garlic and cook until softened.
4. Add the minced beef to the pan and cook

until browned, breaking it up with a spoon as it cooks.
5. Add the cooked quinoa, diced tomatoes, dried oregano, and dried basil to the pan. Season with salt and pepper to taste. Cook for another 5 minutes, stirring occasionally.
6. Remove the pan from the heat and stir in the crumbled feta cheese.
7. Stuff the bell peppers with the quinoa and beef mixture. Place the stuffed bell peppers in the Instant Vortex Plus Versa Zone.
8. Bake for 30-35 minutes, or until the peppers are tender and the filling is golden brown.
9. Serve hot, garnished with fresh parsley. Enjoy

Lentil Soup

Pressure cook

Serves: 6
Prep time: 10 minutes
Cook time: 25 minutes

Ingredients:

- 250g dried lentils, rinsed and drained
- 1 onion, chopped
- 2 garlic cloves, minced
- 1 large carrot, peeled and chopped
- 1 celery stalk, chopped
- 1 potato, peeled and chopped
- 1 bay leaf
- 1 teaspoon dried thyme
- 1 teaspoon paprika
- 1 liter vegetable or chicken broth
- 250ml water
- Salt and pepper to taste
- Fresh parsley, chopped (optional)

Instructions:

1. Add the lentils, onion, garlic, carrot, celery, potato, bay leaf, thyme, paprika, vegetable or chicken broth, and water to the Instant Vortex Plus Versa Zone at 180°c
2. Close the lid and set the Instant Vortex Plus Versa Zone to pressure cook on high for 20 minutes.
3. Once the pressure cooking cycle is complete, let the pressure release naturally for 5 minutes before releasing the remaining pressure manually.
4. Open the lid and discard the bay leaf. Season the soup with salt and pepper to taste.
5. If you prefer a smoother consistency, use an immersion blender to puree the soup until it reaches your desired consistency.
6. Serve hot and garnish with chopped fresh parsley, if desired

CHAPTER 4: APPETIZERS

Irish Colcannon (Cál Ceannann)

Prep time: 10 minutes
Cook time: 20 minutes
Serves 4

Ingredients
- 1kg white potatoes, peeled and cut into bite-sized chunks
- 1 small head of Savoy cabbage, cut into large wedges
- 1 tsp olive oil
- Sea salt and cayenne pepper, to taste
- 4 tbsp butter
- 150ml double cream
- 2 spring onions, finely chopped

Instructions
1. Slide the tray divider into the cooking tray. Put the cooking basket into the Air Fryer and then, press the Control Dial two times quickly to activate Dual Zone cooking.
2. Toss potatoes and cabbage with olive oil, salt, and pepper.
3. Lower the potatoes into Drawer 1 of your Air Fryer. Select "Air Fry" on this drawer and set the temperature to 190 degrees C and the time to 20 minutes.
4. Place the cabbage in Drawer 2. Select "Air Fry", and set the temperature to 190 degrees C and the time to 10 minutes. Select "SyncFinish" to ensure both drawers finish at the same time.
5. Chop the cabbage. Mash potatoes with butter until uniform and smooth. Warm the cream and, once hot, beat it into your potato mash.
6. Add the cabbage and green onions to the potato mixture. Season to taste and serve warm.
7. Bon appétit!

Sweet Potato Wedges

Prep time: 5 minutes
Cook time: 15 minutes
Serves 5-6

Ingredients
- 1.5kg sweet potatoes, cut into wedges
- 1/2 fresh lemon, juiced
- 1/2 tsp paprika
- Sea salt and ground black pepper, to taste
- 1/4 tsp ground coriander
- 1/2 tsp garlic powder
- 1 tsp olive oil
- Dipping Sauce:
- 150ml mayonnaise
- 1 tbsp Cajun seasoning
- 1 tbsp tomato paste
- 1 tsp onion powder
- 1/2 tsp garlic powder

Instructions
1. Toss sweet potato wedges with the other Ingredients. Lower sweet potato wedges into the Air Fryer cooking basket.
2. Select "Air Fry" and set the time for 15 minutes and the temperature to 200 degrees C.
3. When the display shows "Turn Food", shake the basket to ensure even cooking; insert the cooking basket again to continue cooking.
4. Meanwhile, whisk the sauce Ingredients until everything is well combined. Place in your fridge until ready to serve.
5. Taste and adjust the seasoning. Serve with the chilled dipping sauce on the side.
6. Bon appétit!

Devils on Horseback

Prep time: 10 minutes
Cook time: 10 minutes
Serves 10

Ingredients

- 20 walnut halves
- Sea salt flakes, to taste
- 20 whole dates, pitted
- 10 rashers of smoked streaky bacon

Instructions

1. Season the walnuts with sea salt and, then stuff them inside the dates. Halve the rashers of bacon across the middle.
2. Wrap each stuffed date in a piece of bacon and secure them with cocktail sticks. Now, lower the devils into the Air Fryer cooking basket.
3. Select "Air Fry" and set the time for 10 minutes and the temperature to 190 degrees C.
4. When the display shows "Turn Food", turn the devils over to ensure even cooking; insert the cooking basket again to continue cooking.
5. Serve with your favourite dipping sauce and enjoy!

Sausage Rolls

Prep time: 10 minutes
Cook time: 12 minutes
Serves 6

Ingredients

- 375 g rolled puff pastry sheet
- 400g sausage meat
- 1 tbsp English mustard
- 1 medium egg, beaten

Instructions

1. Cut the puff pastry sheet into 3 equal horizontal slices. Divide the sausage meat and mustard between puff pastry slices. (You can mould sausage meat into a cylindrical shape if desired).
2. Now, fold one edge of the pastry over the meat and roll it up. Use a fork to seal the edges together.
3. After that, cut each roll into 6 to 8 pieces; brush them with the beaten egg and lower them onto the Air Fryer cooking basket.
4. Select "Bake" and set the time for 12 minutes and the temperature to 200 degrees C.
5. Leave sausage to cool on a wire rack for 7 to 8 minutes before serving. Enjoy!

British Beef Crostini

Prep time: 10 minutes
Cook time: 14 minutes
Serves 6

Ingredients

- 600g beef fillet, sliced
- 1 tbsp olive oil
- 1 tsp dried basil
- 1 tsp English mustard powder
- Sea salt and ground black pepper, to taste
- 1 large baguette, sliced diagonally
- 200ml double cream
- 2 tbsp chives, snipped
- 200g cheese spread, slightly softened
- 1 handful arugula (Rocket)

Instructions

1. Slide the tray divider into the cooking tray. Put the cooking basket into the Air Fryer and then, press the Control Dial two times quickly to activate Dual Zone cooking.
2. Rub the beef slices with the oil, basil, mustard, salt, and pepper; lower them into Drawer 1 of your Air Fryer. Select "Air Fry" on this drawer and set the temperature to 200 degrees C and the time to 14 minutes.

3. Place the baguette slices in Drawer 2. Select "Bake", and set the temperature to 170 degrees C and the time to 6 minutes. Select "SyncFinish" to ensure both drawers finish at the same time.
4. In the meantime, thoroughly combine double cream with chives and cheese spread. Keep in the fridge until ready to serve.
5. Just before serving, top the crostini with slices of beef, dollops of the creamy cheese mixture, and arugula leaves. Enjoy!

Roasted Brussels Sprouts

Prep time: 5 minutes
Cook time: 10 minutes
Serves 5

Ingredients

- 1kg Brussels sprouts, trimmed and halved
- Sea salt and ground black pepper, to taste
- 1/2 tsp cayenne pepper
- 1/2 tsp dried dill weed
- 1 tsp olive oil
- Dipping Sauce:
- 150g cheddar cheese, freshly grated
- 60ml milk
- 1 tbsp cornstarch
- 1/2 tsp garlic powder
- 1/2 tsp dried parsley flakes

Instructions

1. Toss Brussels sprouts with salt, pepper, dill, and olive oil.
2. Add Brussels sprouts to the Air Fryer cooking basket. Select "Roast" and set the time for 10 minutes and the temperature to 190 degrees C.
3. Heat the cheddar cheese, milk, cornstarch, garlic powder, and parsley flakes in a saucepan over medium heat. Stir continuously for about 5 minutes, until the sauce has thickened.
4. Serve warm Brussels sprouts with the sauce on the side. Enjoy!

Hot Spinach and Artichoke Dip

Prep time: 10 minutes
Cook time: 22 minutes
Serves 8-9

Ingredients

- 4 medium artichokes
- 1 small lemon, juiced
- 1 tsp olive oil
- 1/2 tsp dried basil
- 1 tsp dried parsley flakes
- 1 tsp hot paprika
- Sea salt and ground black pepper, to taste
- 200g cream cheese, softened
- 50g mayonnaise
- 50g Gruyère cheese, grated
- 1 clove garlic, peeled and minced
- Sea salt and ground black pepper, to taste
- 100g frozen chopped spinach, thawed and drained

Instructions

1. Prepare your artichokes: Trim the stems and remove the tough leaves. Cut them in half lengthwise and discard the chokes.
2. Toss your artichokes with lemon juice, olive oil, and spices. Place your artichokes cut side down in the Air Fryer cooking basket.
3. Select "Roast" and set the time for 12 minutes and the temperature to 170 degrees C.
4. Chop your artichokes and add them to a lightly greased casserole dish. Add the other Ingredients and stir to combine well.
5. Add the casserole dish to your Air Fryer. Select "Bake" and set the time for 10 minutes and the temperature to 180 degrees C.
6. Enjoy!

Bourbon Bacon

Prep time: 10 minutes
Cook time: 10 minutes
Serves 6

Ingredients

- 12 rashers double-smoked, thick-cut bacon
- 1/4 cup honey
- 2 tbsp bourbon
- A pinch of ground cloves
- Ground black pepper, to taste

Instructions

1. Toss the bacon with the other Ingredients until well coated on all sides.
2. Arrange bacon slices in the Air Fryer cooking basket. Select "Air Fry" and set the time for 10 minutes and the temperature to 190 degrees C.
3. When the display shows "Turn Food", turn the bacon rashers over to promote even cooking. Insert the basket again to continue cooking.
4. Serv with cocktail sticks and enjoy!

Roasted Asparagus Salad

Prep time: 10 minutes
Cook time: 10 minutes
Serves 4

Ingredients

- 1kg asparagus, trimmed
- 2 tsp olive oil
- Sea salt and ground black pepper, to taste
- 200g cherry tomatoes, halved
- 2 bell peppers, sliced
- 1 small red onion, thinly sliced
- 1 head Romaine lettuce, torn into bite-size pieces
- 1 avocado, sliced
- 1 garlic clove, minced (or 2 chopped spring onion stalks)
- 2 tbsp fresh basil, chopped
- 4 tbsp fresh chives, snipped
- 2 tbsp apple cider vinegar

Instructions

1. Slide the tray divider into the cooking tray. Put the cooking basket into the Air Fryer and then, press the Control Dial two times quickly to activate Dual Zone cooking.
2. Toss asparagus with 1 teaspoon of olive oil, salt, and black pepper; lower the asparagus into Drawer 1 of your Air Fryer.
3. Select "Roast" on this drawer and set the temperature to 200 degrees C and the time to 10 minutes.
4. Toss cherry tomatoes and bell peppers with 1 teaspoon of olive oil; salt and pepper to taste. Place cherry tomatoes and bell peppers in Drawer 2. Select "SyncCook" to automatically mirror the settings in Drawer 2.
5. When the display shows "Turn Food", shake the cooking basket. Insert the cooking basket again to continue cooking.
6. In a nice salad bowl, toss roasted vegetables with the other Ingredients.
7. Bon appétit!

Angels on Horseback

Prep time: 10 minutes
Cook time: 10 minutes
Serves 4

Ingredients

- 14 oysters, shucked
- Sea salt and freshly ground black pepper, to taste
- 7 rashers of smoked bacon
- 1/2 tsp smoked paprika
- 2 tsp dried parsley flakes

Instructions

1. Season the oysters with sea salt and black

pepper. Halve the rashers of bacon across the middle.
2. Wrap each oyster in a piece of bacon and secure them with cocktail sticks. Sprinkle smoked paprika and parsley flakes over them.
3. Now, lower the angels into the Air Fryer cooking basket.
4. Select "Air Fry" and set the time for 10 minutes and the temperature to 190 degrees C.
5. When the display shows "Turn Food", turn the angels over to ensure even cooking; insert the cooking basket again to continue cooking.
6. Serve with your favourite dipping sauce and enjoy!

Welsh Rarebit

Prep time: 10 minutes
Cook time: 10 minutes
Serves 4

Ingredients
- 20g butter
- 30g oat flour
- 200ml stout
- 200g Stilton, grated
- 1 tbsp Worcestershire sauce
- 2 tbsp fresh chives, snipped
- 4 large slices of sourdough bread

Instructions
1. In a saucepan, melt the butter over moderately high heat. Now, tip in the oat flour and stir continuously for about 1 minute.
2. Whisk in the stout; continue whisking for a further 3 minutes, until the sauce has thickened slightly. Fold in the cheese and Worcestershire. Stir again until everything is well incorporated.
3. Arrange bread slices in the Air Fryer cooking basket. Select "Air Fry" and set the time for 6 minutes and the temperature to 200 degrees C.
4. When the display shows "Turn Food", flip the bread slices over and spread them with the stout cheese sauce.
5. Reinsert the cooking basket to continue cooking. Garnish with fresh chives and serve warm. Enjoy!

Cheese & Onion Pasty

Prep time: 10 minutes + chilling time
Cook time: 30 minutes
Serves 4

Ingredients
- Pastry
- 200g cold butter, cubed
- 350g plain flour
- 50ml cold milk
- 1 tsp salt
- 2 medium eggs, beaten

Filling:
- 1 tbsp olive oil unsalted butter
- 1 medium onion, chopped
- 200g cheddar cheese, grated
- 2 tbsp cream cheese, optional

Instructions
1. Using your fingertips, rub the butter into the flour until the mixture resembles fine breadcrumbs.
2. Now, blend in cold milk, salt, and 1 egg to make a firm dough. Cut equally into 4 pieces and chill them for about 30 minutes.
3. In a bowl, thoroughly combine all the filling Ingredients; salt and pepper to taste.
4. On a lightly floured surface, roll out each piece of dough into rounds the size of a tea plate.
5. Divide the filling between pastry circles. Brush the pastry with the remaining beaten egg. Fold the circle in half over the filling and seal the edges. Brush them with the remaining beaten egg.
6. Select "Bake" and set the time for 10 minutes

and the temperature to 200 degrees C. Then, lower the temperature to 180 degrees and cook for 20 minutes more until golden.
7. Bon appétit!

Leeks in Cheese Sauce

Prep time: 10 minutes
Cook time: 20 minutes
Serves 5-6

Ingredients
- 30g butter, room temperature
- 500g leeks, and cut into 2cm chunks
- 40g oat flour
- 400ml full-fat milk
- 1 tsp dried parsley flakes
- 1 tsp dried basil
- 100g cheddar cheese, grated
- 50g breadcrumbs

Instructions
1. Brush the inside of an ovenproof baking dish with 1 teaspoon of butter.
2. In a mixing bowl, thoroughly combine the leeks, flour, milk, parsley, basil, and the remaining butter.
3. Tip the mixture into the prepared baking dish. Scatter over the cheese and breadcrumbs, and lower the dish into the Air Fryer cooking basket.
4. Select "Bake" and set the time for 20 minutes and the temperature to 190 degrees C.
5. When the display shows "Turn Food", rotate the dish to promote even cooking; reinsert the cooking basket and continue to bake until it is golden on top and hot, bubbling at the edges. Enjoy!

Stilton and Walnut Tarts

Prep time: 10 minutes
Cook time: 20 minutes
Serves 6

Ingredients
- 1 tbsp olive oil
- 375g pack of ready-rolled puff pastry
- 1 tbsp butter, room temperature
- 2 large shallots, sliced
- 2 tbsp thyme leaf
- Zest and juice of 1 lemon
- 150g Stilton cheese
- 50g walnut halves, chopped

Instructions
1. Brush the inside of 4 tart tins with olive oil.
2. Unroll the pastry and then, cut 4 circles of approximately the same size as your tart tins. Press the dough into the greased tins. Prick the dough with a fork.
3. In a mixing bowl, thoroughly combine the butter, shallots, thyme, lemon zest and juice. Spread the shallot mixture on top of the pastry, within the border.
4. Crumble over the cheese and scatter with the chopped walnuts.
5. Select "Bake" and set the time for 20 minutes and the temperature to 200 degrees C.
6. When the display shows "Turn Food", rotate the tarts to promote even cooking; reinsert the cooking basket and continue to bake until golden and puffed. Enjoy!

Spicy Baked Camembert

Prep time: 10 minutes
Cook time: 15 minutes
Serves 4-5

Ingredients
- 300g camembert
- 1 tbsp dry vermouth
- 1 rosemary sprig
- 1 tsp red chilli flakes
- 4 thick slices of bread
- 2 garlic cloves, peeled

Instructions

1. Slide the tray divider into the cooking tray. Put the cooking basket into the Air Fryer and then, press the Control Dial two times quickly to activate Dual Zone cooking.
2. Toss your camembert with vermouth, rosemary, and chilli flakes. Now, lower your camembert into Drawer 1 of your Air Fryer.
3. Select "Bake" on this drawer and set the temperature to 200 degrees C and the time to 15 minutes.
4. Place the bread slices in Drawer 2. Select "Bake", and set the temperature to 170 degrees C and the time to 6 minutes. Select "SyncFinish" to ensure both drawers finish at the same time.
5. When the display shows "Turn Food", turn the bread slices over. Reinsert the cooking basket to continue cooking.
6. Rub toasted bread slices with garlic. Serve baked camembert with toasted garlicky bread. Devour!

Easy Corn Fritters

Prep time: 10 minutes + chilling time
Cook time: 20 minutes
Serves 4

Ingredients

Corn Fritters:
- 200g can sweetcorn, drained
- 1 tbsp fresh parsley, chopped
- 1 medium carrot, grated
- 1 shallot, chopped
- 1 tsp smoked paprika
- 60g self-raising flour
- 1 egg
- 1 tsp English mustard
- 4 tbsp full-fat milk
- 4 tbsp tomato paste
- 1 tbsp olive oil

Sauce:
- 100ml mayonnaise
- 1 small gherkin finely chopped
- 1 tsp garlic granules
- 1 tsp dried oregano

Instructions

1. Thoroughly combine all Ingredients for corn fritters.
2. Shape the mixture into patties and place them in your fridge for about 30 minutes.
3. Once chilled, transfer the corn patties to a lightly greased Air Fryer cooking basket.
4. Select "Air Fry" and set the time for 20 minutes and the temperature to 180 degrees C.
5. Meanwhile, whisk the sauce Ingredients in a bowl; place the sauce in the fridge until ready to serve.
6. When the display shows "Turn Food", turn corn fritters over to promote even cooking; reinsert the cooking basket and continue frying until thoroughly cooked.
7. Serve warm corn fritters with chilled sauce on the side. Enjoy!

Classic British Faggots

Prep time: 10 minutes
Cook time: 10 minutes
Serves 8

Ingredients

- 300g pork shoulder
- 100g pig's heart or liver
- 100g bacon, cut into small chunks
- 100 grams breadcrumbs
- 1 medium onion, finely chopped
- 2 tbsp fresh basil leaves, chopped
- 2 tbsp fresh parsley, chopped
- 1 tsp chilli pepper
- Salt and freshly ground black pepper, to taste
- 8 rashers of streaky bacon, sliced in half lengthwise

Instructions

1. Pulse the meat and 100g of bacon in your food processor until coarsely chopped.
2. To make British faggots, thoroughly combine the meat with bacon chunks, breadcrumbs, onion, herbs, and spices.
3. Now, shape the mixture into 16 large faggots and wrap each ball in a bacon slice; use toothpicks to secure, if needed. *(freeze at this point if needed)*
4. Lower the prepared meatballs into the lightly greased Air Fryer basket.
5. Select "Air Fry" and set the time for 10 minutes and the temperature to 175 degrees C.
6. When the display shows "Turn Food", turn your faggots over to promote even cooking; reinsert the cooking basket.
7. When the faggots have reached 71 degrees C, they're done.
8. Serve with cocktail sticks and enjoy!

Mashed Peppery Turnips

Prep time: 10 minutes
Cook time: 12 minutes
Serves 4-5

Ingredients

- 1kg turnips, peeled and cut into but-sized chunks
- 1 tsp olive oil
- Sea salt and ground black pepper, to taste
- 2 tbsp double cream
- 1 tbsp butter
- 1 tbsp fresh coriander, finely chopped
- 1 tsp garlic powder
- 1/2 tsp chilli powder

Instructions

1. Toss turnip chunks with olive oil, salt, and black pepper. Add turnip to the lightly greased Air Fryer cooking basket.
2. Select "Air Fry" and set the time for 12 minutes and the temperature to 200 degrees C.
3. When the display shows "Turn Food", shake the basket to promote even cooking. Reinsert the cooking basket to continue cooking.
4. Then, mash warm turnip with double cream, butter, and spices; salt to taste and enjoy!

Spicy Parmesan Wafers

Prep time: 5 minutes
Cook time: 2 minutes
Serves 5-6

Ingredients

- 200g parmesan cheese, grated
- 1 tsp hot paprika
- 1/2 tsp garlic granules
- 1/2 tsp dried basil

Instructions

1. Line a baking tray with a piece of baking paper; set it aside.
2. Thoroughly combine parmesan cheese with paprika garlic, and basil.
3. Place 1 tbsp piles of cheese mixture on the lined baking tray leaving a 1 cm space between them. Make sure to flatten each pile slightly using a spoon (or a rolling pin).
4. Add the baking tray to the cooking basket. Select "Air Fry" and set the time for 2 minutes and the temperature to 190 degrees C.
5. There is no need to turn your food. Cool until crisp and enjoy!

Roasted Root Vegetables

Prep time: 5 minutes
Cook time: 12 minutes
Serves 5-6

Ingredients

- 1kg carrots, peeled and sliced
- 1/2kg celery root, peeled and sliced

- 1kg turnip, cut into wedges
- Sea salt and ground black pepper, to taste
- 1 tsp cayenne pepper
- 1/2 tsp dried basil
- 1/2 tsp dried oregano
- 1 tsp sweet paprika (optional)
- 1 tbsp olive oil
- Dipping Sauce:
- 100ml mayonnaise
- 50g cream cheese
- 2 tbsp fresh chives, snipped

Instructions

1. Slide the tray divider into the cooking tray. Put the cooking basket into the Air Fryer and then, press the Control Dial two times quickly to activate Dual Zone cooking.
2. Toss your vegetables with spices and olive oil until well coated on all sides.
3. Arrange carrots and celery in Drawer 1 of your Air Fryer. Select "Roast" on this drawer and set the temperature to 200 degrees C and the time to 12 minutes. Place the turnip wedges in Drawer 2.
4. Select "SyncCook" to automatically mirror the settings in Drawer 2. When the display shows "Turn Food", shake the cooking basket. Insert the basket again to continue cooking until cooked through.
5. In the meantime, thoroughly combine all Ingredients for the sauce. Keep in the fridge until ready to serve.
6. Serve warm root vegetables with the chilled sauce on the side. Bon appétit!

Petite Perfectly Topped Pizza

Serves: 2
Prep time: 15 minutes
Cook time: 15-20 minutes

Ingredients:

- All-purpose flour (60g)
- Teaspoon instant yeast (2g)
- Teaspoon salt (1g)
- Teaspoon sugar (1g)
- lukewarm water (60ml)
- Tablespoon olive oil (7ml)
- pizza sauce (60ml)
- shredded mozzarella cheese (60g)
- Toppings of your choice (such as sliced mushrooms, chopped bell peppers, sliced onions, etc.)

Instructions

1. Preheat your Instant Vortex Plus Versa Zone temperature to 200°C.
2. In a mixing bowl, combine the all-purpose flour, instant yeast, salt, and sugar. Add in the lukewarm water and olive oil, and stir until a dough forms.
3. Knead the dough on a floured surface for 3-5 minutes, until it becomes smooth and elastic.
4. Divide the dough into 2 equal portions, and roll each portion into a circle with a diameter of about 15 cm.
5. Place the dough circles on a baking sheet or pizza stone, and spread each with pizza sauce.
6. Sprinkle shredded mozzarella cheese on top of each pizza, and add your desired toppings.
7. Place the baking sheet or pizza stone into the Instant Vortex Plus Versa Zone and cook for 15-20 minutes, or until the cheese is melted and bubbly and the crust is golden brown.
8. Remove the pizzas from the oven, slice and serve hot. Enjoy!

Movie Night Crunchy Popcorn

Serves: 4
Prep time: 5 minutes
Cook time: 15 minutes

Ingredients:

- 100g popcorn kernels
- 50g unsalted butter

- 50ml honey
- 25ml vegetable oil
- 1 tsp salt
- 50g peanuts
- 50g M&Ms

Instructions

1. Preheat the Instant Vortex Plus Versa Zone to 180°C.
2. Add the popcorn kernels and vegetable oil to the Instant Vortex Plus Versa Zone and set the timer for 15 minutes.
3. Melt the unsalted butter in a saucepan over low heat. Once melted, add the honey and stir until combined.
4. Once the popcorn is done popping, transfer it to a large mixing bowl.
5. Pour the melted butter and honey mixture over the popcorn and stir until the popcorn is evenly coated.
6. Add the peanuts and M&Ms to the bowl and mix until evenly distributed.
7. Serve the Movie Night Crunchy Popcorn Mix immediately or store in an airtight container for later

Deliciously Stuffed Ravioli Bites

Serves: 4
Prep time: 10 minutes
Cook Time: 20 minutes

Ingredients:

- 400g fresh or frozen ravioli
- 200g ricotta cheese
- 100g grated Parmesan cheese
- 1 egg
- 50g chopped fresh parsley
- 1 tsp salt
- 1/2 tsp black pepper
- 100g bread crumbs
- 50ml olive oil

Instructions

1. Preheat the Instant Vortex Plus Versa Zone to 180°C.
2. In a mixing bowl, combine the ricotta cheese, Parmesan cheese, egg, chopped parsley, salt, and black pepper. Mix well.
3. Lay the ravioli out on a flat surface and spoon a small amount of the cheese mixture onto each one.
4. Fold the ravioli in half and press the edges together to seal the filling inside.
5. Place the bread crumbs into a shallow dish. Coat each ravioli bite in bread crumbs, pressing gently to ensure they are evenly coated.
6. Drizzle the olive oil over the ravioli bites and place them into the Instant Vortex Plus Versa Zone.
7. Bake for 20 minutes or until the ravioli bites are golden brown and crispy.

Glazed Heavenly Donut Rings

Serves: 12 donut rings
Prep time: 15 minutes
Cook time: 10 minutes

Ingredients:

- 400g all-purpose flour
- 100g granulated sugar
- 2 tsp baking powder
- 1/2 tsp baking soda
- 1/2 tsp salt
- 240ml buttermilk
- 2 large eggs
- 60ml vegetable oil
- 1 tsp vanilla extract
- 120ml hot water
- Vegetable oil for frying

For the Glaze:

- 250g icing sugar

- 60ml milk
- 1 tsp vanilla extract

Instructions

1. Preheat the Instant Vortex Plus Versa Zone temperature to 175°C.
2. In a large mixing bowl, whisk together the flour, sugar, baking powder, baking soda, and salt until combined.
3. In a separate mixing bowl, whisk together the buttermilk, eggs, vegetable oil, and vanilla extract until smooth.
4. Pour the wet Ingredients into the dry Ingredients and mix until just combined. Add hot water and mix again until you get a smooth batter.
5. Grease a donut pan with vegetable oil and fill each mold halfway with the batter.
6. Place the donut pan into the Instant Vortex Plus Versa Zone and bake for 8-10 minutes or until golden brown and fully cooked.
7. Remove the donut pan from the oven and allow the donut rings to cool down for 5-10 minutes before removing them from the pan.
8. In a mixing bowl, whisk together the icing sugar, milk, and vanilla extract until you get a smooth glaze.
9. Dip the top of each donut ring into the glaze and let it drip off any excess. Place the donut rings onto a wire rack to set.
10. Allow the glaze to set for a few minutes before serving. Enjoy your delicious Glazed Heavenly Donut Rings!

Creamy Tzatziki Dip Recipe

Serves: 4-6
Prep time: 10 minutes
Cook time: 0 minutes

Ingredients:

- (250 ml) plain Greek yogurt
- 1 small cucumber, seeded and grated
- 1 clove garlic, minced
- 1 tablespoon (15 ml) lemon juice
- 1 tablespoon (15 ml) olive oil
- 1 teaspoon (5 g) salt
- 1/2 teaspoon (2 g) black pepper
- 1 tablespoon (5 g) fresh dill, chopped
- 1 tablespoon (5 g) fresh mint, chopped

Instructions

1. preheat Instant Vortex Plus Versa Zone to 4°c
2. In a medium-sized mixing bowl, combine the Greek yogurt, grated cucumber, minced garlic, lemon juice, olive oil, salt, and black pepper. Stir well to combine and place in the Instant Vortex
3. Add the fresh dill and fresh mint to the yogurt mixture and stir again until all Ingredients are evenly distributed.
4. Transfer the mixture to a serving bowl and chill in the refrigerator for at least 30 minutes to allow the flavors to meld together.
5. Once chilled, give the dip a quick stir and serve with pita bread, vegetables, or chips.

Crispy Bread and Butter Pickles

Serves: 6-8
Prep time : 1 hour
cook time :10-15 minutes

Ingredients:

- 800g cucumbers, sliced
- 1 onion, sliced
- 3 cloves garlic, minced
- 500 ml white vinegar
- 250 ml water
- 250 g granulated sugar
- 2 tbsp pickling salt
- 1 tbsp mustard seeds
- 1 tsp turmeric
- 1 tsp celery seeds

Instructions

1. In a large bowl, mix together the cucumbers, onion, and garlic.
2. In a medium saucepan, combine the vinegar, water, sugar, pickling salt, mustard seeds, turmeric, and celery seeds. Heat the mixture over medium heat until the sugar has dissolved.
3. Pour the vinegar mixture over the cucumber mixture and stir to combine.
4. Cover the bowl and refrigerate for at least 1 hour, or overnight.
5. Preheat the Instant Vortex Plus Versa Zone Temperature to 190°C.
6. Spread the pickles out in a single layer on the Instant Vortex Fry Tray and Air Fry for 10-15 minutes, or until crispy and golden brown.
7. Serve immediately.

Bite-Sized Bagel Delights

Serves: 4-6
Prep time: 15 minutes
Cook time: 20-25 minutes

Ingredients:

- 4 plain bagels, cut into small bite-sized pieces
- 60 ml olive oil
- 2 cloves garlic, minced
- 2 tsp dried oregano
- 1/2 tsp salt
- 1/4 tsp black pepper
- 100 g cream cheese, softened
- 30 g parmesan cheese, grated
- 60 ml sour cream
- 60 ml mayonnaise
- 60 ml milk
- 1 tbsp fresh parsley, chopped
- 1 tbsp fresh chives, chopped

Instructions

1. Preheat the Instant Vortex Plus Versa Zone to 190°C.
2. In a small bowl, combine the olive oil, minced garlic, dried oregano, salt, and black pepper.
3. Place the bagel pieces in a large mixing bowl and pour the seasoned olive oil over the top. Toss until the bagel pieces are well coated.
4. Spread the bagel pieces out in a single layer on the baking tray in the Instant Vortex Plus Versa Zone. Cook for 10-12 minutes, flipping the bagel pieces halfway through, until they are crispy and golden brown.
5. While the bagel pieces are cooking, prepare the dip by combining the cream cheese, parmesan cheese, sour cream, mayonnaise, milk, parsley, and chives in a medium-sized mixing bowl. Whisk until the mixture is smooth and creamy.
6. Once the bagel pieces are done, remove them from the Instant Vortex Plus Versa Zone and allow them to cool for a few minutes.
7. Serve the Bite-Sized Bagel Delights with the creamy dip on the side for dipping. Enjoy

Crispy Golden Onion Blossoms

Serves : 4-6
Prep time: 10 minutes
Cook time: 15-20 minutes

Ingredients:

- 1 large onion
- 240 ml all-purpose flour
- 2 tsp paprika
- 1 tsp garlic powder
- 1 tsp salt
- 1/2 tsp black pepper
- 240 ml milk

- 2 eggs
- 240 ml panko breadcrumbs

Instructions

1. Preheat the Instant Vortex Plus Versa Zone to 190°C.
2. Peel the onion and cut off the stem end. Place the onion on a cutting board with the flat end facing down. Cut the onion into 1/2-inch thick wedges, making sure to leave about 1/2 inch at the bottom of the onion intact so that the petals stay connected.
3. In a shallow bowl, mix together the flour, paprika, garlic powder, salt, and black pepper.
4. In another shallow bowl, whisk together the milk and eggs.
5. In a third shallow bowl, place the panko breadcrumbs.
6. Dip each onion wedge into the flour mixture, making sure to coat the entire onion. Shake off any excess flour.
7. Dip the onion wedge into the milk and egg mixture, making sure to coat the entire onion.
8. Finally, dip the onion wedge into the panko breadcrumbs, pressing the breadcrumbs onto the onion to make sure it is well coated.
9. Place the onion wedges onto the baking tray in the Instant Vortex Plus Versa Zone. Cook for 15-20 minutes, or until the onion is crispy and golden brown.
10. Once the onion is cooked, remove it from the Instant Vortex Plus Versa Zone and allow it to cool for a few minutes.
11. To serve, place the Crispy Golden Onion Blossom onto a plate and gently separate the petals to create a blossom shape. Serve with your favorite dipping sauce, such as ranch or chipotle mayo. Enjoy!

Crispy Golden Rice Balls

Serves :4-6
Prep time: 30 minutes
Cook Time: 15-20 minutes

Ingredients:

- 300ml uncooked white rice
- 500ml water
- 1 teaspoon salt
- 2 tablespoons butter
- Grated Parmesan cheese
- 2 tablespoons chopped fresh parsley
- 2 eggs, beaten
- 1 cup breadcrumbs
- Salt and pepper, to taste
- Oil for frying

Instructions

1. Rinse the rice in a fine-mesh strainer and place it in a pot with 2 cups of water and 1 teaspoon of salt. Bring to a boil, reduce the heat to low, cover, and simmer for 18-20 minutes or until the rice is fully cooked.
2. Once the rice is cooked, add the butter, Parmesan cheese, and chopped parsley. Mix well until the butter is melted and the cheese is melted and evenly distributed throughout the rice.
3. Allow the rice mixture to cool to room temperature, then form into small balls, about 1-2 tablespoons each.
4. Preheat the Instant Vortex Plus Versa Zone Temperature to 190°C.
5. Beat the eggs in a bowl and set aside.
6. Place the breadcrumbs in a separate bowl and season with salt and pepper to taste.
7. Dip each rice ball into the beaten egg, then roll it in the seasoned breadcrumbs until fully coated.
8. Place the rice balls onto the Instant Vortex Plus Versa Zone Temperature baking tray,

spaced evenly apart and at 180°c
9. Lightly drizzle or spray the rice balls with oil.
10. Bake for 15-20 minutes, or until the rice balls are crispy and golden brown.

Savory Bacon-Wrapped Dates

Serves: 12
Prep time: 15 minutes
Cook time: 15-20 minutes

Ingredients:
- 12 Medjool dates, pitted
- 6 slices of bacon, cut in half
- Goat cheese
- Almonds, chopped
- 1 tbsp honey
- Salt and pepper, to taste

Instructions
1. Preheat the Instant Vortex Plus Versa Zone temperature to 200°C
2. In a small bowl, mix together the goat cheese, chopped almonds, honey, and a pinch of salt and pepper.
3. Stuff each date with the goat cheese mixture.
4. Wrap each date with a half slice of bacon and secure with a toothpick.
5. Place the wrapped dates in the Instant Vlrtex Plus fryer basket in a single layer, and cook at 200 degrees Celsius for 15-20 minutes or until the bacon is crispy.
6. Once done, remove from the Instant Vortex Plus fryer and let cool for a few minutes before serving.

Bite-Sized Quiche Delights

Serves : 24 mini quiches
Prep time: 20 minutes.
Cook time: 20-25 minutes

Ingredients:
- 200g all-purpose flour
- 100g unsalted butter, chilled and diced
- 1 egg yolk
- 2-3 tablespoons cold water
- 100g smoked bacon, diced
- 1/2 onion, diced
- 2 eggs
- 150ml heavy cream
- 50g grated Parmesan cheese
- Salt and pepper to taste

Instructions
1. Preheat the Instant Vortex Plus Versa Zone to 190°C.
2. In a large mixing bowl, combine the flour and diced butter. Use your fingertips to rub the butter into the flour until the mixture resembles breadcrumbs.
3. Add the egg yolk and cold water to the mixture and mix until a dough forms. Knead the dough for a few minutes until it is smooth, then wrap it in plastic wrap and chill it in the fridge for at least 10 minutes.
4. Roll out the chilled dough on a floured surface until it is about 3mm thick. Use a round cookie cutter to cut out circles of dough and press them into a greased mini muffin tin.
5. In a pan, cook the diced bacon and onion until the bacon is crispy and the onion is translucent. Set aside to cool.
6. In a mixing bowl, whisk together the eggs, heavy cream, grated Parmesan cheese, salt, and pepper until well combined.
7. Divide the bacon and onion mixture evenly among the mini quiches, then pour the egg mixture over the top.
8. Bake the mini quiches in the preheated oven for 20-25 minutes or until the egg mixture is set and the pastry is golden brown.
9. Remove the mini quiches from the oven and

allow them to cool for a few minutes before removing them from the muffin tin. Serve warm or at room temperature

Irresistible Mini Corn Dogs

Serves: 20 mini corn dogs
Prep time: 20 minutes
Cook time: 10-12 minutes

Ingredients:

- 1 cup (125g) yellow cornmeal
- 1 cup (125g) all-purpose flour
- 1 tablespoon baking powder
- 1/4 teaspoon salt
- 1/4 teaspoon black pepper
- 1 tablespoon sugar
- 1 egg, beaten
- 240ml milk
- 2 tablespoons vegetable oil
- 20 mini hot dogs
- Wooden skewers
- Ketchup and mustard, for serving

Instructions

1. Preheat the Instant Vortex Plus Versa Zone to 190°C.
2. In a large mixing bowl, whisk together the cornmeal, flour, baking powder, salt, black pepper, and sugar.
3. In another mixing bowl, whisk together the beaten egg, milk, and vegetable oil until well combined.
4. Add the wet Ingredients to the dry Ingredients and mix until just combined. Do not overmix.
5. Insert a wooden skewer into each mini hot dog.
6. Dip each hot dog into the batter, making sure it is coated evenly.
7. Place the battered hot dogs onto the Instant Vortex Plus Versa Zone air fryer basket or air fryer tray in a single layer.
8. Air fry the mini corn dogs for 10-12 minutes or until they are golden brown and cooked through, flipping them halfway through cooking.
9. Serve the mini corn dogs with ketchup and mustard on the side

Flaky Puff Pastry Pigs in a Blanket

Serves: 24 mini pigs in a blanket
Prep time: 20 minutes
Cook time: 12-15 minutes

Ingredients:

- 1 sheet of puff pastry, thawed
- 24 cocktail sausages
- 1 egg, beaten
- Sesame seeds, for sprinkling (optional)
- Ketchup and mustard, for serving

Instructions

1. Preheat the Instant Vortex Plus Versa Zone to 190°C.
2. Cut the puff pastry sheet into 24 equal strips.
3. Wrap each cocktail sausage in a strip of puff pastry, making sure to pinch the edges to seal the pastry around the sausage.
4. Brush the beaten egg over the top of each wrapped sausage and sprinkle with sesame seeds (if desired).
5. Place the wrapped sausages onto the Instant Vortex Plus Versa Zone air fryer basket or air fryer tray in a single layer.
6. Air fry the pigs in a blanket for 12-15 minutes or until the pastry is golden brown and puffed up.
7. Serve the pigs in a blanket with ketchup and mustard on the side

Spicy Cheesy Jalapeno Poppers

Serves: 12 jalapeno poppers
Prep time: 20 minutes
Cook time: 8-10 minutes

Ingredients:
- 6 jalapeno peppers
- 60g cream cheese, softened
- 60g shredded cheddar cheese
- 1/4 teaspoon garlic powder
- 1/4 teaspoon paprika
- Salt and pepper, to taste
- 1 egg, beaten
- 60g breadcrumbs
- Cooking spray

Instructions
1. Preheat the Instant Vortex Plus Versa Zone to 190°C.
2. Cut the jalapeno peppers in half lengthwise and remove the seeds and membranes.
3. In a mixing bowl, combine the softened cream cheese, shredded cheddar cheese, garlic powder, paprika, salt, and pepper.
4. Spoon the cheese mixture into each jalapeno half, filling them evenly.
5. In a shallow bowl, beat the egg.
6. Place the breadcrumbs in another shallow bowl.
7. Dip each stuffed jalapeno half into the beaten egg, then coat it with breadcrumbs.
8. Spray the Instant Vortex Plus Versa Zone air fryer basket or air fryer tray with cooking spray.
9. Place the coated jalapeno halves onto the air fryer basket or tray in a single layer.
10. Air fry the jalapeno poppers for 8-10 minutes or until the breadcrumbs are golden brown and the cheese is melted and bubbly.
11. Serve the jalapeno poppers immediately

Crispy Seasoned Tater Tots

Serves: 4
Prep time: 5 minutes
Cook time: 15-20 minutes

Ingredients:
- 450g frozen tater tots
- 2 tablespoons olive oil
- 1 teaspoon garlic powder
- 1 teaspoon paprika
- 1/2 teaspoon salt
- 1/4 teaspoon black pepper

Instructions
1. Preheat the Instant Vortex Plus Versa Zone to 200°C.
2. In a large mixing bowl, combine the frozen tater tots, olive oil, garlic powder, paprika, salt, and black pepper.
3. Toss the tater tots with the seasoning mixture until they are evenly coated.
4. Spray the Instant Vortex Plus Versa Zone air fryer basket or air fryer tray with cooking spray.
5. Place the seasoned tater tots onto the air fryer basket or tray in a single layer.
6. Air fry the tater tots for 15-20 minutes or until they are crispy and golden brown, shaking the basket or tray halfway through cooking to ensure even browning.
7. Remove the tater tots from the Instant Vortex Plus Versa Zone and serve immediately

CHAPTER 5: BRITISH CLASSIC

Rustic pub-style feast

Serves: 2-4
Prep time: 15 minutes
Cook Time: 15 minutes

Ingredients:
- 500g mixed cheese (cheddar, Stilton, and or Red Leicester), sliced or cubed
- 200g cooked ham, sliced
- 200g pickled onions
- 200g sliced bread
- 100g butter, softened
- 50g Dijon mustard
- 30ml apple cider vinegar
- 30ml olive oil
- 5g salt
- 5g black pepper
- 1 apple, cored and sliced
- 1 celery stick, sliced
- 1 carrot, peeled and sliced

Instructions:
1. Preheat the Instant Vortex Plus Versa Zone to 180°C.
2. Arrange the cheese, ham, and pickled onions on a baking tray and place in the preheated Instant Vortex Plus Versa Zone for 10-15 minutes, until the cheese is melted and bubbly.
3. Meanwhile, in a small bowl, whisk together the softened butter, Dijon mustard, apple cider vinegar, olive oil, salt, and black pepper to make the dressing.
4. Toast the sliced bread in a toaster or on a grill until lightly browned.
5. To serve, divide the cheese, ham, and pickled onions between serving plates. Add the sliced apple, celery, and carrot to the plates. Drizzle the dressing over everything and serve with the toasted bread.

Hearty hand-held pie

Serves: 4
Prep time: 30 minutes
Cook Time: 45 minutes

Ingredients:
- 500g beef mince
- 300g potatoes, peeled and diced
- 200g swede, peeled and diced
- 100g onion, diced
- 1 tsp dried thyme
- 1 tsp dried rosemary
- Salt and pepper to taste
- 350g shortcrust pastry
- 1 egg, beaten
- Cooking spray or oil

Instructions:
1. Preheat the Instant Vortex Plus Versa Zone to 200°C.
2. In a large mixing bowl, combine the beef mince, diced potatoes, swede, onion, thyme, rosemary, salt, and pepper. Mix well.
3. Roll out the shortcrust pastry on a floured surface and cut into four equal squares.
4. Divide the beef and vegetable mixture evenly between the four squares, placing the mixture on one half of each square.
5. Brush the edges of each square with the beaten egg, then fold the other half of the pastry over the mixture to form a triangle. Press the edges together to seal.
6. Spray the Instant Vortex Plus Versa Zone basket with cooking spray or brush with oil. Place the pasties in the basket, making sure

they don't touch each other.
7. Brush the tops of the pasties with more beaten egg.
8. Cook the pasties in the Instant Vortex Plus Versa Zone for 45 minutes, or until they are golden brown and the filling is cooked through.
9. Serve hot with your favorite sauce or gravy. Enjoy!

Fragrant, spicy Indian curry

airfryer & Microwave

Serves: 4
Prep time: 30 minutes
Cook Time: 25 minutes

Ingredients:

For the Marinade:
- 500g boneless, skinless chicken breast, cut into 1-inch pieces
- 150g plain yogurt
- 2 cloves garlic, minced
- 1 tsp grated ginger
- 1 tsp ground cumin
- 1 tsp ground coriander
- 1 tsp smoked paprika
- 1/2 tsp ground turmeric
- Salt and pepper to taste

For the Sauce:
- 2 tbsp ghee or vegetable oil
- 1 onion, chopped
- 3 cloves garlic, minced
- 1 tbsp grated ginger
- 1 tbsp tomato paste
- 1 tbsp garam masala
- 1 tsp ground cumin
- 1 tsp ground coriander
- 1/2 tsp turmeric
- 400g can of chopped tomatoes
- 120ml heavy cream
- Salt and pepper to taste
- Fresh cilantro for garnish

Instructions:

1. In a large mixing bowl, combine the chicken pieces with the marinade Ingredients. Mix well to ensure the chicken is fully coated. Cover and refrigerate for at least 30 minutes.
2. Preheat the Instant Vortex Plus Versa Zone to 200°C.
3. Place the marinated chicken pieces on the Instant fryer basket and place it in the Instant Vortex Plus Versa Zone. Cook for 10-12 minutes or until the chicken is fully cooked through and has a slightly charred appearance.
4. While the chicken is cooking, make the sauce. In a large saucepan, heat the ghee or vegetable oil over medium heat. Add the onion and cook until softened, about 5 minutes.
5. Add the garlic and ginger and cook for another minute, stirring constantly.
6. Add the tomato paste, garam masala, cumin, coriander, turmeric, and canned tomatoes to the pan. Stir well to combine.
7. Bring the mixture to a simmer and cook for 10-15 minutes, stirring occasionally, until the sauce has thickened and reduced slightly.
8. Once the chicken is cooked, add it to the pan with the sauce and stir to combine.
9. Add the heavy cream to the pan and stir well. Season with salt and pepper to taste.
10. Let the mixture simmer for another 2-3 minutes to allow the flavors to blend together.
11. Serve hot, garnished with fresh cilantro leaves. Enjoy with naan bread or rice on the side.

Comforting lamb and potato casserole

Serves: 6
Prep time: 30 minutes
Cook Time: 1 hour 30 minutes

Ingredients:
- 800g lamb shoulder, trimmed and cut into bite-sized pieces
- 2 tbsp plain flour
- Salt and pepper to taste
- 2 tbsp olive oil
- 2 onions, chopped
- 3 carrots, peeled and sliced
- 3 potatoes, peeled and sliced
- 1 bay leaf
- 1 tsp dried thyme
- 500ml beef broth
- 2 tbsp Worcestershire sauce
- 1 tbsp tomato paste
- 50g butter, melted
- 1 large egg, beaten
- Cooking spray or oil

Instructions:
1. Preheat the Instant Vortex Plus Versa Zone to 160°C.
2. In a large mixing bowl, season the lamb pieces with salt and pepper, then toss with the plain flour until fully coated.
3. Heat the olive oil in a large skillet over medium-high heat. Brown the lamb pieces on all sides in the skillet, then transfer to a large casserole dish.
4. Add the chopped onions and sliced carrots to the skillet and cook until softened, about 5 minutes. Transfer to the casserole dish with the lamb.
5. Arrange the sliced potatoes on top of the lamb and vegetables in the casserole dish, overlapping them slightly.
6. Add the bay leaf and dried thyme to the casserole dish.
7. In a small bowl, mix together the beef broth, Worcestershire sauce, tomato paste, melted butter, and beaten egg. Pour the mixture over the potatoes in the casserole dish.
8. Spray the Instant Vortex Plus Versa Zone basket with cooking spray or brush with oil. Place the casserole dish in the basket, making sure it doesn't touch the sides.
9. Cover the casserole dish with foil, then cook in the Instant Vortex Plus Versa Zone for 1 hour and 30 minutes, or until the lamb is tender and the potatoes are fully cooked.
10. Remove the foil from the casserole dish and turn the Instant Vortex Plus Versa Zone temperature up to 200°C. Return the casserole dish to the basket and cook for another 10-15 minutes or until the top is golden brown and crispy.
11. Let the Lancashire Hotpot cool for a few minutes before serving. Enjoy!

Elegant, savory pastry-wrapped steak

Serves: 4
Prep time: 45 minutes
Cook Time: 45 minutes

Ingredients:
- 500g beef fillet, trimmed
- Salt and pepper to taste
- 2 tbsp olive oil
- 2 tbsp Dijon mustard
- 2 sheets of puff pastry, thawed
- 100g prosciutto, sliced
- 150g mushrooms, finely chopped
- 1 garlic clove, minced
- 1 tbsp fresh thyme leaves, chopped
- 50g butter
- 1 large egg, beaten

- Cooking spray or oil

Instructions:

1. Preheat the Instant Vortex Plus Versa Zone to 200°C.
2. Season the beef fillet with salt and pepper.
3. Heat the olive oil in a skillet over high heat. Sear the beef fillet on all sides until browned, then remove from the skillet and let it cool down for a few minutes.
4. Brush the beef fillet with Dijon mustard and set it aside.
5. In the same skillet, sauté the prosciutto, mushrooms, garlic, and thyme in butter until the mushrooms are soft and any liquid has evaporated. Let the mixture cool down.
6. On a lightly floured surface, roll out each puff pastry sheet to approximately 30x30cm.
7. Place a sheet of puff pastry on a baking sheet lined with parchment paper or sprayed with cooking spray.
8. Spread the mushroom mixture evenly over the pastry sheet, leaving a border around the edges.
9. Place the seared beef fillet on top of the mushroom mixture.
10. Wrap the puff pastry around the beef fillet and brush the edges with beaten egg to seal.
11. Place the beef Wellington in the Instant Vortex Plus Versa Zone basket sprayed with cooking spray or brushed with oil.
12. Brush the top of the puff pastry with beaten egg and make a few small slits on top to allow steam to escape.
13. Cook the beef Wellington for approximately 45 minutes, or until the internal temperature reaches 54°C for medium-rare or 60°C for medium.
14. Let the beef Wellington rest for a few minutes before slicing and serving. Enjoy!

Toad in the hole

Serves: 4
Prep time: 10 minutes
Cook Time: 30 minutes

Ingredients:

- 8 sausages
- 150g all-purpose flour
- 1/2 tsp salt
- 2 large eggs
- 300ml whole milk
- 2 tbsp vegetable oil

Instructions:

1. Preheat the Instant Vortex Plus Versa Zone to 220°C.
2. Place the sausages in a baking dish and bake them in the preheated Vortex Plus Versa Zone for 10-15 minutes until browned on all sides.
3. While the sausages are cooking, mix the flour and salt in a large mixing bowl.
4. Add the eggs and whisk together until a smooth batter is formed.
5. Gradually add the milk while continuing to whisk until the batter is well combined.
6. Let the batter rest for 10 minutes.
7. After the sausages are browned, remove the baking dish from the oven and pour the vegetable oil over the sausages.
8. Pour the batter over the sausages, making sure they are completely covered.
9. Return the baking dish to the Instant Vortex Plus Versa Zone and cook for an additional 20-25 minutes until the batter is risen and golden brown.
10. Serve hot with your favorite sides. Enjoy your Toad in the Hole!

Yorkshire Pudding

Serves: 6
Prep time: 10 minutes
Cook Time: 20 minutes

Ingredients:

- 100g all-purpose flour
- 2 large eggs
- 125ml whole milk
- 125ml water
- 1/2 tsp salt
- 2 tbsp vegetable oil

Instructions:

1. Preheat the Instant Vortex Plus Versa Zone to 220°C.
2. In a medium bowl, whisk together the flour and salt.
3. In a separate bowl, beat the eggs until frothy.
4. Gradually add the milk and water to the eggs while whisking continuously.
5. Slowly pour the egg mixture into the bowl with the flour mixture while whisking until well combined and smooth.
6. Add the vegetable oil to the Versa Zone and heat for 2-3 minutes, until the oil is hot.
7. Carefully pour the batter into the hot oil in the Versa Zone.
8. Bake for 20 minutes, or until the Yorkshire pudding is golden brown and crispy on the outside.
9. Remove the Yorkshire pudding from the Versa Zone and serve immediately.
10. Enjoy your delicious Yorkshire pudding!

Rich, hearty Irish comfort food

[handwritten note: ? How to cook this possibly microwave or pressure cooker]

Serves: 4-6
Prep time: 20 minutes
Cook Time: 50 minutes

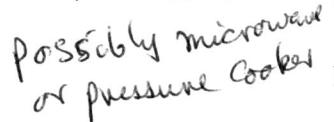

Ingredients:

- 800g beef chuck roast, cut into 2-inch pieces
- 2 tbsp all-purpose flour
- 1 tsp salt
- 1/2 tsp black pepper
- 2 tbsp vegetable oil
- 1 medium onion, chopped
- 3 garlic cloves, minced
- 2 celery stalks, chopped
- 2 large carrots, chopped
- 2 tbsp tomato paste
- 375ml beef broth
- 375ml Guinness beer
- 1 bay leaf
- 1 tsp dried thyme

Instructions:

1. In a large bowl, combine the flour, salt, and black pepper. Add the beef and toss to coat.
2. Preheat the Instant Vortex Plus Versa Zone to 190°C.
3. Add the vegetable oil to the Versa Zone and heat for 2-3 minutes.
4. Add the beef to the Versa Zone and brown on all sides, working in batches if necessary. Remove the beef from the Versa Zone and set aside.
5. Add the onion, garlic, celery, and carrots to the Versa Zone and sauté for 2-3 minutes, until the vegetables begin to soften.
6. Add the tomato paste and stir to combine.
7. Add the beef broth, Guinness beer, bay leaf, and thyme to the Versa Zone and stir to combine.
8. Return the beef to the Versa Zone and stir to combine with the sauce.
9. Cover the Versa Zone with the lid and cook for 40-45 minutes, or until the beef is tender and the sauce has thickened.
10. Remove the bay leaf and serve the Beef and Guinness Stew hot.
11. Enjoy your delicious Beef and Guinness Stew!

Whipped cream and berry delight

Serves: 4
Prep time: 10 minutes
Cook Time: 10 minutes

Ingredients:

- 150g fresh strawberries, chopped
- 150g fresh raspberries
- 2 tbsp caster sugar
- 200ml heavy cream
- 50g meringue cookies, crushed

Instructions:

1. Preheat the Instant Vortex Plus Versa Zone to 200°C.
2. In a medium bowl, combine the chopped strawberries, raspberries, and caster sugar. Mix well and set aside.
3. Add the heavy cream to a large bowl and whisk until stiff peaks form.
4. Gently fold the berry mixture into the whipped cream.
5. Add the crushed meringue cookies to the mixture and fold gently to combine.
6. Spoon the Eton Mess into serving glasses.
7. Place the glasses in the Versa Zone and bake for 5-10 minutes, or until the tops of the Eton Mess have browned slightly.
8. Remove the glasses from the Versa Zone and serve the Eton Mess immediately.

Sticky Toffee Pudding

Serves: 6
Prep time: 20 minutes
Cook Time: 30-35 minutes

Ingredients:

- 200g pitted dates, chopped
- 250ml boiling water
- 1 tsp bicarbonate of soda
- 85g unsalted butter, softened
- 175g caster sugar
- 2 large eggs
- 200g self-raising flour, sifted
- 1 tsp vanilla extract

For the Toffee Sauce:

- 100g unsalted butter
- 200g soft brown sugar
- 150ml double cream

Instructions:

1. Preheat your Instant Vortex Plus Versa Zone to 180°C.
2. Place the chopped dates in a bowl and pour over the boiling water. Stir in the bicarbonate of soda and leave to one side.
3. In a separate bowl, cream together the softened butter and caster sugar until light and fluffy. Beat in the eggs, one at a time, then fold in the flour and vanilla extract.
4. Pour the date mixture into the bowl with the butter and sugar mixture, and stir together until well combined.
5. Grease a 20cm cake tin with butter and pour the mixture into the tin, spreading it out evenly
6. Place the cake tin into the Instant Vortex Plus Versa Zone and bake for 30-35 minutes, or until a skewer inserted into the centre comes out clean.
7. While the pudding is baking, make the toffee sauce. Melt the butter and brown sugar together in a saucepan over a low heat. Add the double cream and stir until the mixture is smooth and combined.
8. Once the pudding is cooked, remove it from the oven and allow it to cool for a few minutes.
9. Turn the pudding out onto a serving dish and pour the toffee sauce over the top.
10. Serve the Sticky Toffee Pudding with a

dollop of whipped cream or a scoop of vanilla ice cream, if desired

Buttery, crumbly tea-time treat

scones (handwritten)

Serves: 8
Prep time: 15 minutes
Cook Time: 10-12 minutes

Ingredients:

- 350g self-raising flour
- 85g unsalted butter, chilled and cubed
- 3 tbsp caster sugar
- 175ml milk
- 1 tsp vanilla extract
- 1 large egg, beaten

Instructions:

1. Preheat your Instant Vortex Plus Versa Zone to 220°C.
2. In a large bowl, rub the chilled butter cubes into the self-raising flour until the mixture resembles breadcrumbs.
3. Stir in the caster sugar.
4. In a separate jug, mix together the milk, vanilla extract and beaten egg.
5. Make a well in the centre of the dry Ingredients and pour in the wet Ingredients.
6. Mix together with a knife until the mixture forms a soft dough.
7. Turn the dough out onto a lightly floured surface and knead lightly until smooth.
8. Roll out the dough to a thickness of about 2cm and use a 5cm round cutter to cut out the scones.
9. Place the scones onto a lined baking tray and brush the tops with a little bit of milk.
10. Place the tray into the Instant Vortex Plus Versa Zone and bake for 10-12 minutes, or until the scones are risen and golden.
11. Remove the tray from the oven and allow the scones to cool for a few minutes before serving.
12. Serve the scones warm with your favourite jam and clotted cream, or butter and honey.

Moist, tangy citrus dessert

Serves: 8
Prep time: 15 minutes
Cook Time: 30 minutes

Ingredients:

For the cake:
- 175g unsalted butter, softened
- 175g caster sugar
- 3 large eggs
- 175g self-raising flour
- 1 tsp baking powder
- 2 tbsp milk
- Zest of 1 lemon

For the drizzle:
- 100g granulated sugar
- Juice of 1 lemon

Instructions:

1. Preheat the Instant Vortex Plus Versa Zone to 180°C.
2. In a mixing bowl, cream together the butter and sugar until light and fluffy.
3. Beat in the eggs one at a time, making sure to mix well after each addition.
4. Sift the flour and baking powder into the mixing bowl and fold until just combined.
5. Stir in the milk and lemon zest.
6. Grease a 20cm round cake tin and spoon in the cake batter, smoothing the surface.
7. Place the cake tin in the Instant Vortex Plus Versa Zone and bake for 25-30 minutes, or until a skewer inserted into the center comes out clean.
8. While the cake is baking, make the drizzle by whisking together the sugar and lemon

juice.
9. Remove the cake from the Instant Vortex Plus Versa Zone and leave it in the tin. Prick the surface of the cake all over with a skewer.
10. Pour the drizzle over the cake while it is still warm, making sure to cover the entire surface.
11. Leave the cake to cool completely in the tin before removing and serving

Almond and raspberry Tart pastry perfection

Serves: 8
Prep time: 30 minutes
Cook Time: 50 minutes

Ingredients:

For the Pastry:
- 200g plain flour
- 100g unsalted butter, cubed
- 50g caster sugar
- 1 egg yolk
- 2 tbsp cold water

For the Filling:
- 150g unsalted butter, softened
- 150g caster sugar
- 3 large eggs
- 150g ground almonds
- 1 tsp almond extract
- 1 tbsp plain flour
- 150g raspberry jam

For the Topping:
- 50g flaked almonds

Instructions:

1. Preheat the Instant Vortex Plus Versa Zone to 180°C.
2. To make the pastry, mix the flour and butter in a food processor until the mixture resembles breadcrumbs. Add the sugar, egg yolk, and water, and pulse until the dough comes together. Wrap the pastry in cling film and chill for 30 minutes.
3. Roll out the pastry on a floured surface and use it to line a 23cm tart tin. Prick the base with a fork and chill for another 10 minutes.
4. Line the pastry case with baking paper and fill with baking beans. Blind bake for 10 minutes, then remove the beans and paper and bake for another 5 minutes until the pastry is lightly golden. Remove from the oven and let cool.
5. To make the filling, beat the butter and sugar together until light and fluffy. Beat in the eggs one at a time, then stir in the ground almonds, almond extract, and flour.
6. Spread the raspberry jam over the cooled pastry base. Spoon the almond filling over the jam and smooth the surface.
7. Sprinkle the flaked almonds over the top of the tart.
8. Bake in the Instant Vortex Plus Versa Zone for 35-40 minutes until the filling is set and the almonds are golden.
9. Remove from the oven and let cool before serving. Enjoy your delicious Bakewell Tart made

Classic steamed pudding with a playful name

Serves: 4
Prep time: 15 minutes
Cook Time: 30 minutes

Ingredients:

- 225g self-raising flour
- 100g shredded suet
- 75g caster sugar
- 75g currants
- 1 large egg
- 125ml milk

- 1 tsp vanilla extract
- 1/2 tsp ground cinnamon
- 1/4 tsp ground nutmeg

For the Custard:
- 300ml double cream
- 3 large egg yolks
- 25g caster sugar
- 1 tsp vanilla extract

Instructions:

1. In a large mixing bowl, combine the flour, suet, sugar, currants, cinnamon, and nutmeg. Mix well to combine.
2. In a separate mixing bowl, whisk together the egg, milk, and vanilla extract. Pour the wet Ingredients into the dry Ingredients and mix until well combined.
3. Grease a heat-proof dish that will fit inside the Instant Vortex Plus Versa Zone. Spoon the batter into the dish and smooth the surface.
4. Cover the dish with aluminum foil, making sure to leave a little space for the pudding to expand. Place the dish in the Instant Vortex Plus Versa Zone.
5. Select the Bake function and set the temperature to 180°C. Set the timer for 30 minutes.
6. While the pudding is baking, make the custard. In a saucepan, heat the cream over medium heat until it begins to steam.
7. In a mixing bowl, whisk together the egg yolks, sugar, and vanilla extract. Slowly pour the hot cream into the egg mixture, whisking constantly to combine.
8. Return the custard mixture to the saucepan and cook over low heat, stirring constantly, until it thickens enough to coat the back of a spoon.
9. Remove the pudding from the Instant Vortex Plus Versa Zone and let it cool for a few minutes.
10. Serve the pudding warm with the custard spooned over the top.

CHAPTER 6: DESSERTS

Apple Charlotte

Prep time: 10 minutes
Cook time: 35 minutes
Serves 6-8

Ingredients
- 120g unsalted butter, melted, plus extra for the basin
- 2 tbsp golden caster sugar
- 8 slices white bread, remove the crust

Filling:
- 60g cold unsalted butter, room temperature
- 160g caster sugar
- 1 large apple, peeled, cored and cut into 1cm pieces
- 1 tbsp lemon juice
- A pinch of sea salt
- 1/4 tsp ground cloves
- 1 tsp cinnamon

Instructions
1. Lightly butter a pudding basin and dust with 2 tablespoons of golden caster sugar.
2. Flatten the bread slices with a rolling pin. Dip the bread slices in the melted butter and line the base and sides of the basin with half of them. Place the pudding basin in the fridge.
3. Next, make the filling; melt the butter and sugar in a large saucepan over moderately high heat until it turns a dark caramel colour. Add the apples, lemon juice and spices and continue to cook for a further 6 minutes, until the liquid has reduced slightly.
4. Spoon the apple filling into the pudding basin. Cover with the remaining bread and press down the edges. Add the pudding basin to the Air Fryer basket.
5. Select "Bake" and set the time for 35 minutes and the temperature to 190 degrees C.
6. Leave to cool for 5 minutes before removing from the pudding basin. Serve with ice cream and enjoy!

British Jaffa Cakes

Prep time: 10 minutes + chilling time
Cook time: 15 minutes
Serves 6

Ingredients
- 1 tbsp butter
- 1 medium egg
- 3 tbsp caster sugar
- 3 tbsp self-raising flour
- 1 tsp ground cinnamon
- 1/2 tsp vanilla extract
- 1 medium orange, zested
- 130g dark chocolate

Orange jelly:
- 150g pack of orange jelly, cut into cubes
- 50ml fresh orange juice

Instructions
1. Butter a 12-hole cupcake tin. In a mixing bowl, beat the egg and sugar using an electric whisk until pale and frothy. Sift over the flour; stir in the cinnamon, vanilla, and orange zest. Mix to combine well.
2. Spoon the batter into the prepared cupcake tin.
3. Lower the cupcake tin into the Air Fryer basket. Select "Bake" and set the time for 10 minutes and the temperature to 180 degrees C; transfer to a wire rack to cool completely.
4. Meanwhile, make the orange jelly. Put the jelly cubes and orange juice in a heatproof

bowl. Add 120ml of boiling water, and stir until the jelly cubes have dissolved. Spoon your jelly into a shallow baking tray and chill for at least 3 hours.
5. Cut chilled jelly into discs. Top each cookie with a jelly disc.
6. Melt dark chocolate in a heatproof bowl in your microwave. Spoon the melted chocolate over the jaffa cakes and leave to set for about 5 minutes. Bon appétit!

Mini Christmas Puddings

Prep time: 10 minutes
Cook time: 25 minutes
Serves 6-8

Ingredients
- 1 tbsp butter
- 1 tbsp golden caster sugar
- 200g dried currants
- 20 grams mixed candied fruit peel, finely chopped
- 100ml brandy
- 50ml fresh orange juice
- Zest of 1 orange
- 1 large carrot, grated
- 220g cookie crumbs
- 60g treacle
- 200g self-rising flour
- 230g vegetarian suet
- 2 large eggs, lightly beaten
- 230g brown sugar
- 1 tsp ground cloves
- 1 tsp ground cinnamon

Instructions
1. Butter 4-5 ramekins; dust them with 1 tablespoon of sugar and set them aside.
2. Place the dried fruits, candied peel, brandy, and orange juices in a bowl; stir to combine. Cover the bowl with a tea towel and let it stand for a couple of hours.
3. Add the dry Ingredients and mix to combine well. Beat in the egg and add the liquid Ingredients; beat to combine well.
4. Scrape the batter into the prepared ramekins, gently pressing the mixture down to distribute evenly. Cover with a thin layer of foil.
5. Select "Bake" and set the time for 25 minutes and the temperature to 160 degrees C. When the display shows "Turn Food", remove the foil. Insert the basket again to continue cooking until golden brown on the top.
6. Bon appétit!

Classic Yorkies (Yorkshire Puddings)

Prep time: 10 minutes
Cook time: 20 minutes
Serves 6-8

Ingredients
- 1 tsp butter, melted
- 140g plain flour
- 1/2 tsp sea salt
- 4 medium eggs
- 250 ml milk

Instructions
1. Butter Yorkshire pudding tins and set them aside.
2. Tip plain flour into a mixing bowl along with sea salt.
3. Now, beat in the eggs. Slowly and gradually whisk in milk. Continue mixing until everything is well incorporated.
4. Pour the batter into a jug, then remove the hot tins from the oven. Carefully and evenly pour the batter into the holes.
5. Place the tins in the Air Fryer cooking basket. Select "Bake" and set the time for 20

minutes and the temperature to 190 degrees C. When the display shows "Turn Food", rotate the tins to promote even cooking.
6. Insert the basket again to continue cooking until the puddings have puffed up.
7. Bon appétit!

Christmas Cake with Brandy Sauce

Prep time: 10 minutes
Cook time: 25 minutes
Serves 10

Ingredients

Cake:
- 250g soft bread crumbs
- 100g raisins
- 100g cup dried currants
- 100g prunes, pitted and chopped
- 2 medium apples, cored, peeled and shredded
- 50ml brandy
- 50g maraschino cherries
- 50g walnuts, chopped
- 100g red candied cherries
- 50g cup butter, softened
- 100g cup packed brown sugar
- 2 medium eggs
- 100g self-raising flour
- 1 tsp baking soda
- A pinch of sea salt
- A pinch of ground cloves
- 50ml cup orange juice

Sauce:
- 50g cup brown sugar
- 50ml cup butter, cubed
- 1 egg yolk
- 50ml double cream
- 2 tbsp brandy

Instructions

1. Lightly grease a baking tin and set it aside.
2. To make the cake: add the dry Ingredients to a mixing bowl; mix to combine well. Beat in the egg and add the liquid Ingredients; beat to combine well.
3. Scrape the batter into the prepared baking tin, gently pressing the mixture down to distribute evenly. Cover with a thin layer of foil.
4. Select "Bake" and set the time for 25 minutes and the temperature to 160 degrees C. When the display shows "Turn Food", remove the foil. Insert the basket again to continue cooking until golden brown on the top.
5. Meanwhile, in a saucepan, combine the brown sugar, butter, egg yolk, and cream. Bring to a rapid boil and continue to cook, whisking continuously for about 2 minutes, until the sauce has thickened.
6. Pour in brandy, stir to combine, and remove from the heat. Pour the hot sauce into a jug, and keep warm until serving time.
7. Slide a palette knife all around the cake to make it easy to turn it out onto a serving tray. Afterwards, poke holes in the cake with a skewer and spoon over the warm brandy sauce. Leave the cake to cool completely.
8. Bon appétit!

Grandma's Apple Crumble

Prep time: 10 minutes
Cook time: 35 minutes
Serves 8-9

Ingredients

Filling:
- 3 medium apples, peeled, cored and cut into 1cm slices
- 1 tbsp lemon juice
- 2 tbsp honey

Crumble:
- 185g oat flour

- 100g golden caster sugar
- A pinch of sea salt
- A pinch of ground cloves
- 1 tsp ground cinnamon
- 100g cold butter

Instructions

1. Toss your apples with lemon juice and honey; arrange them on a baking tray.
2. In a mixing bowl, thoroughly combine the flour with golden caster sugar, sea salt, ground cloves, and cinnamon.
3. Slice in cold butter; then, rub it in with your fingertips until it looks like moist breadcrumbs.
4. Scrape the crumb mixture over the apples and gently press the surface with the back of the spoon.
5. Put in the preheated Air Fryer. Select "Bake" and set the time for 35 minutes and the temperature to 180 degrees C. When the display shows "Turn Food", rotate the baking tray. Insert the basket again to continue cooking until golden brown on the top.
6. Serve with clotted cream or custard, if desired. Enjoy!

Bread and Butter Pudding

Prep time: 1 hour 10 minutes
Cook time: 30 minutes
Serves 8

Ingredients

- 300ml full-fat milk
- 250ml double cream
- 1 tsp vanilla extract
- 3 large eggs
- 4 tbsp honey
- 9 slices of day-old crusty bread, torn into pieces
- 40g coconut oil, room temperature
- 100g mix of dried currants (or prunes)
- Zest of 1
- 2 lemon
- 2 tbsp golden caster sugar

Instructions

1. To make the custard, in a deep saucepan, bring the milk, cream and vanilla to a boil. Whisk the eggs until pale and fluffy; add in the honey and mix again to combine well.
2. Now, gradually pour the warm custard, over the eggs, stirring constantly until smooth.
3. Lightly oil an ovenproof baking dish with coconut oil. Lay half of the bread pieces in the bottom of the dish. Scatter the dried fruit, the remaining coconut oil, and lemon zest over the bread. Layer the rest of the bread.
4. Spoon the custard mixture over the bread and leave to soak for about 1 hour.
5. Select "Bake" and set the time for 30 minutes and the temperature to 160 degrees C.
6. Bon appétit!

Traditional Yorkshire Parkin

Prep time: 10 minutes
Cook time: 35 minutes
Serves 8

Ingredients

- 100g unsalted butter, softened
- 100g coconut oil, room temperature
- 50ml treacle
- 100g brown sugar
- 200ml golden syrup
- 200 g self-rising flour
- 100g porridge oatmeal
- 1 tsp pumpkin pie spice
- 1 tsp baking powder
- 2 large eggs, beaten
- 2 tbsp plain milk, if needed

Instructions

1. In a mixing bowl, thoroughly combine all dry Ingredients. Then, in a separate bowl, mix all wet Ingredients.
2. Add the wet mixture to the dry Ingredients; mix to combine well. Scrape the mixture into a lightly greased baking tray and add it to the Air Fryer cooking basket.
3. Select "Bake" and set the time for 35 minutes and the temperature to 160 degrees C.
4. When the display shows "Turn Food", rotate the baking tray. Reinsert the basket to continue cooking until golden brown on the top.
5. Bon appétit!

The Easiest Eccles Cakes Ever

Prep time: 10 minutes + chilling time
Cook time: 20 minutes
Serves 8

Ingredients

Pastry:
- 230g plain flour
- A pinch of flaky sea salt
- 180g butter, very cold

Filling:
- 60g butter
- 120g golden caster sugar
- 60g mixed candied fruit peel, finely chopped
- 180g currants
- Zest of 1 large lemon
- 1/4 tsp grated nutmeg
- 1 tsp ground cinnamon
- 1 egg white, beaten

Instructions

1. Tip the flour into a mixing bowl with a pinch of sea salt. Now, coarsely grate the butter straight into the bowl. Use a cutlery knife to stir; pour in 130ml of cold water to bring the dough together. Let it chill for 30 minutes in your fridge.
2. Make the filling: melt the butter along with sugar, candied fruit peel, currants, lemon zest, nutmeg, and cinnamon.
3. On a lightly floured working surface, roll out the chilled dough. Cut into 6-8 circles and divide the filling between them. Pull up the edges and pinch to seal.
4. Beat the egg white with a fork until fluffy. Brush the egg white over the tops of the cakes. Arrange them on a parchment-lined baking sheet.
5. Select "Bake" and set the time for 20 minutes and the temperature to 180 degrees C.
6. When the display shows "Turn Food", rotate the baking tray. Reinsert the basket to continue cooking. Bon appétit!

Sticky Toffee Pudding

Prep time: 10 minutes
Cook time: 30 minutes
Serves 6-8

Ingredients

Pudding:
- 85g butter, softened
- 170g self-raising flour
- 1 tsp bicarbonate of soda
- 1/2 tsp vanilla extract
- 1/2 tsp ground cumin
- 2 medium eggs
- 140g brown sugar
- 2 tbsp molasses
- 100ml plain milk
- 220g fresh dates, pitted, chopped, and soaked in 170ml of boiling water for 20 min

Sauce:
- 170g golden caster sugar
- 60g butter, cut into pieces

- 220ml double cream
- 1 tbsp molasses

Instructions

1. Butter mini pudding tins and set them aside.
2. In a mixing bowl, thoroughly combine the flour with the bicarbonate of soda, vanilla, and cumin.
3. In another bowl, beat the eggs until pale and frothy. Beat in softened butter and brown sugar until creamy and uniform.
4. Gradually and slowly, pour in molasses and milk. Add the wet mixture to the dry Ingredients; fold in the soaked dates and mix to combine well.
5. Spoon the batter evenly between the pudding tins. Select "Bake" and set the time for 20 minutes and the temperature to 160 degrees C.
6. Meanwhile, in a medium saucepan, heat all the sauce Ingredients. Cook until the sugar has completely dissolved.
7. Remove the puddings from your Air Fryer. Pour the sauce over them.
8. When ready to serve, Select "Reheat" and set the time for 10 minutes and the temperature to 180 degrees C.
9. Bon appétit!

St Clement's Pie

Prep time: 10 minutes
Cook time: 35 minutes
Serves 6

Ingredients

Crust:
- 230g almond meal
- 90g cornflake
- 80g butter, melted
- 120g golden caster sugar

Filling:
- 1 large egg
- 4 large egg yolks
- 380g full-fat coconut milk
- Zest and juice of 2 oranges

Topping:
- 130ml double cream
- 80g Greek yoghurt
- 4 tbsp golden syrup

Instructions

1. Mix all the Ingredients for the crust. Press the crust mixture into the base and sides of a lightly greased baking tin.
2. Select "Bake" and set the time for 15 minutes and the temperature to 160 degrees C.
3. To make the filling, whisk the egg and yolks in a big bowl until pale and frothy. Whisk in the coconut milk, followed by the zests and juices of your oranges. Pour the filling into the tin.
4. Select "Bake" and set the time for 20 minutes and the temperature to 160 degrees C.
5. Whip the cream, Greek yoghurt, and golden syrup. Dollop the cream mixture on the pie and enjoy!

Mini Rhubarb Crumbles

Prep time: 10 minutes
Cook time: 35 minutes
Serves 6

Ingredients

- 400g rhubarb, chopped into bite-sized chunks
- 80g golden caster sugar
- 1 tsp lemon zest
- 2 tbsp brandy

Crumble Topping:
- 130g self-raising flour
- 1 tsp ground cinnamon
- 1/2 tsp anise, ground
- 80g butter, chilled
- 40g brown muscovado sugar

- 2 tbsp raw almonds, slivered

Instructions

1. Cook rhubarb with caster sugar, lemon zest, and brandy for about 10 minutes; divide the rhubarb mixture between lightly greased ramekins.
2. In a mixing bowl, thoroughly combine the topping Ingredients. Scrape the topping mixture over the rhubarb layer and gently press the surface with the back of the spoon.
3. Put the ramekins into the preheated Air Fryer. Select "Bake" and set the time for 35 minutes and the temperature to 180 degrees C.
4. When the display shows "Turn Food", rotate the ramekins to promote even cooking. Insert the basket again to continue cooking until golden brown on the top.
5. Serve with clotted cream or custard, if desired.
6. Bon appétit!

Scottish Shortbread

Prep time: 10 minutes + chilling time
Cook time: 20 minutes
Serves 6-8

Ingredients

- 220g butter, room temperature
- 120g golden caster sugar
- 240g plain flour
- 1/2 tsp flaky sea salt

Instructions

1. Line a baking tin with a piece of baking paper.
2. In a mixing bowl, beat the butter and sugar until creamy, uniform, and smooth.
3. Stir in the flour and salt, and mix to combine well; chill in the fridge for about 30 minutes.
4. Press the dough into the prepared baking tin; mark the dough into 12-16 bars using a sharp knife or a pizza cutter.
5. Select "Bake" and set the time for 20 minutes and the temperature to 170 degrees C.
6. When the display shows "Turn Food", rotate the baking tray to promote even cooking. Insert the basket again to continue cooking until golden and set.
7. Let it cool completely before cutting and serving. Devour!

Easy Banana Muffins

Prep time: 10 minutes
Cook time: 16 minutes
Serves 6

Ingredients

- 230g self-raising flour
- 1 tsp baking powder
- 1/2 tsp bicarbonate of soda
- 1/2 tsp vanilla extract
- 100g caster sugar
- 70g butter, melted
- 2 medium eggs
- 2 ripe bananas, mashed
- 120ml buttermilk
- 2 tbsp walnuts, chopped
- 2 tbsp raisins (optional)

Instructions

1. Lightly grease a 12-hole muffin tin using cooking spray.
2. In a mixing bowl, thoroughly combine the flour, baking powder, bicarb, sugar, and vanilla.
3. In a separate jug, whisk the eggs until pale and frothy. Add the other liquid Ingredients and whisk again. Tip the jug contents into the dry mixture; stir to combine well and gently fold in walnuts and raisins, if using.
4. Divide the batter between muffin holes.

5. Select "Bake" and set the time for 16 minutes and the temperature to 200 degrees C. Leave the muffins to cool for about 10 minutes before unmolding.
6. Bon appétit!

Gooey Raisin Cookies

Prep time: 10 minutes
Cook time: 13 minutes
Serves 8

Ingredients
- 100g raisins
- 50ml dark rum
- 220g unsalted butter, at room temperature
- 150 golden caster sugar
- 1 medium egg
- 250g self-raising flour

Instructions
1. Soak raisins in 50ml of dark rum for about 15 minutes.
2. Beat the butter and sugar until the sugar dissolved. Then, beat in the egg until fluffy.
3. Gradually tip in the flour; mix with an electric whisk until everything is well combined. Fold in the soaked raisins.
4. Spoon the dough onto a lightly greased baking tin in 16 rough blobs.
5. Select "Bake" and set the time for 13 minutes and the temperature to 170 degrees C.
6. Leave the cookies to cool on a wire rack for about 10 minutes.
7. Bon appétit!

Chocolate Brownie Cake

Prep time: 10 minutes
Cook time: 35 minutes
Serves 6-8

Ingredients
- 170g butter
- 220g dark chocolate, broken into chunks
- 100g caster sugar
- 100g golden syrup
- 3 eggs, separated and beaten
- 60g plain flour
- 50g almond meal

Instructions
1. Lightly butter a cake tin and set it aside.
2. Melt the chocolate in your microwave and gradually stir in the other Ingredients. Stir until everything is well incorporated.
3. Scrape the batter into the prepared cake tin and lower the tin into the Air Fryer cooking basket.
4. Select "Bake" and set the time for 35 minutes and the temperature to 160 degrees C.
5. Leave to cool in a tin; after that run a knife around the sides and remove your cake from the tin. Cut your cake into squares and enjoy!

Printed in Great Britain
by Amazon